CATS IN CLOVER

CATS IN CLOVER

By

Lea Tassie

Cats in Clover by Lea Tassie
Copyright © 2004 Lea Tassie

*Publisher's note: This book is a work of fiction. Names, characters, places and incidents are the product of the
author's imagination or are used fictitiously, and any resemblance to actual persons living or dead, events or
locales is entirely coincidental.*

Manufactured in Canada.

Library and Archives Canada Cataloguing in Publication

Tassie, Lea, 1935-
        Cats in clover / Lea Tassie.

Also available in electronic format.
ISBN 1-897098-37-5

        1.Cats—Fiction. I.Title.

PS8589.A8732C38 2004   C813'.6   C2004-903674-2

TreeSide Press
2610 Selwyn Rd.
Victoria, B.C., Canada V9B 3L5
http://www.treesidepress.ca

DEDICATION

To the memory of
Dianne Taylor (1948-1995)

ACKNOWLEDGMENTS

With affectionate thanks to all the Cat People I've known, in particular: Lynn Arnold, Susan McBride, Betty Carmichael, Mayne Ellis, Margaret Holland, Dr. Ken Kowal, Anne Lane, Josie Robertson, June Townley and, most of all, to my husband, Al Tassie.

Last, but certainly not least, thanks to my critics, Ellen Godfrey, Sheryl Dunn, Laura Langston and Judith Todd Monroe, and to my helpful advisor on farms and pools, Derek Chandler.

I - A NEW YEAR, A NEW LIFE

I had to yell to make myself heard over the night club's orchestra and the shouts and laughter of other New Year's Eve revelers. "If you insist we buy a farm, I insist on having at least two or three cats around!"

"I don't want cats on our farm," Ben shouted back across the table. "They're boring and brainless. All they do is sleep and shed hair."

"That's not true! Cats are a lot of fun. And they catch mice. Didn't you listen to all those stories I told you about how funny they are?"

"I listened; I just don't believe it."

This ritual argument had been going on for the entire fifteen years of our marriage. We lived in a condo near Beacon Hill Park and pets weren't allowed but I'd managed to partly assuage my longing for those furry, cuddly, crazy little characters called cats by visiting my Aunt Peggy, who always had two or three in residence.

Now my life was changed completely. Ben had just taken early retirement so he could fulfil his life-long dream of living on a small farm. Aunt Peggy, much to my sorrow, had passed away in November. She'd left me the house but her cats had gone to a friend. I'd tried persuading Ben to move into the house, where I could keep Peggy's cats in their familiar territory and he could have a big garden in the back, but he was determined to have his farm, far away from city noise, traffic and hectic work schedules.

Reluctantly, I'd rented out the house and quit my job. I wouldn't miss the job, but I didn't know how I'd survive without the city, my friends and my bridge group. I had to keep telling myself I'd finally have enough peace and quiet to write the short stories I'd been playing with for years. I wouldn't have to get up early or wear pantyhose. I could have as many cats as I wanted and prove to Ben, once and for all, what wonderful animals they were.

Rusty, who had been Ben's ex-boss for all of five hours, tapped my arm and said, "This farming fantasy of Ben's won't work, you know. You're both city people."

"That's right." Jean, Rusty's wife, shook her head at me. "Holly, you don't have a green thumb; you can't even grow house plants."

That was true. My thumb was so brown it was darn near black. It was Ben who loved gardening and wanted to grow carrots and peas and potatoes, not me.

"I grew up on a farm," I said.

"And I've done a lot of reading," Ben added.

"Doesn't matter." Rusty signalled the waiter for another round of drinks. "You don't have any experience and that's what counts."

"We've agreed to give it two years," Ben said. "If I can't make a go of market gardening, or Holly really can't stand country life, we'll be back."

"I'll bet you're back within a year!"

"Wanna put your money where your mouth is?" Ben winked at me.

"Sure!" Rusty pulled a bill out of his wallet and waved it around. "Fifty bucks says I'm right. And I'll even give you your job back so you can pay me off." He looked at me mournfully. "Best cost accountant I ever had and he's gonna go raise chickens and goats!"

***

Three months later we stood at the gate of our new property on Adriana, a small island in the Strait of Georgia.

"There it is, two hectares of the best soil on the island." Ben beamed as he gave me a hug. "And look at that view!"

"Don't talk to me in metric," I said, "it's five acres." He was right about the view, though.

The land lay on the eastern slope of the central north-south spine of hills, facing the Strait. Fifty yards beyond the maples, cedars and Garry oaks fringing the bottom of our meadow, the sea sparkled blue and serene under the March sun. Robins and sparrows warbled. Crows flapped lazily across the sky and seagulls soared over the beach. The air smelled of new growth and salt sea. I looked at the dilapidated buildings and moaned.

"We'll have the place in shape sooner than you think," Ben said, giving me another squeeze.

The old two-story house was big – at least we could have plenty of company – and I loved the wide front veranda facing the island-dotted sea. I could see myself sitting out there every morning with a mug of coffee, watching sunrise spread gold over the water and listening to the sleepy chirping of birds while I scribbled immortal prose. But not until we fixed the cracked siding and completely renovated the interior. Then there was the back door, which faced the road where we stood and seemed about to fall off its hinges. The chicken house resembled a pile of rubble. The two-foot high lawn was booby-trapped with abandoned iron bedsteads and bits of wire. The orchard looked like it hadn't been pruned since the Second World War.

"I've got it all planned out," Ben said. "Renovating won't be a problem."

I thought he was as overly optimistic about the renovations as he was about my learning to love living on a farm. Mora Bay, the ferry terminal and main town on Adriana, was small and we'd probably have to go to Victoria for major supplies. The five miles of gravel road to Mora Bay, twisting through cedar-scented forest and a scattering of tiny farms, took fifteen minutes and the crossing to Victoria an hour. Add the amount of time it would take to drive to a building supply store, pick up materials and make the trip home and we'd blow a whole day just getting a bag of nails. I reminded myself that clocks didn't matter any more.

Ben had assured me, all through the purchase negotiations, that the house looked worse than it was. He said the structure and plumbing were sound and the only major expense, other than replacing the inner and outer shells, would be some electrical work.

Ben patted my arm. "Come on, Holly, quit worrying. The house is livable."

"Just barely." One burner was gone on the stove, the fridge motor gave a death rattle when it shut off and the linoleum was worn down to the backing. In the first glow of finding affordable land that pleased Ben and a view that consoled me – a little – for leaving the city, I hadn't paid much attention to these little problems. Besides, Ben kept consulting his cost estimates and telling me to look at the big picture. So I had. I'd looked at the meadow and the sea and dreamed of going back to the city. And shut my eyes to that disaster of a house.

But renovating, no matter how tough, had to be less of a pain than my years of being a legal secretary, where the only good thing was the salary. And Ben had agreed to my having one cat. A far cry from the six I wanted, but it was a start.

"Don't forget the pool," he said. "When the weather gets warmer we can have a leisurely dip every night before cocktails. More luxury than we had in the condo."

The real estate agent told us that the pool had been put in six months before, the only new structure on the place. Ben was yearning to strip off the blue plastic cover and dive in but the pool wasn't heated and, even for a water enthusiast like him, March is not the time to go swimming in southern British Columbia. As far as I was concerned, water was only useful as a hot shower or in a glass with ice. A pool was merely something to sit beside with a book, a plate of munchies and a martini.

Footsteps crunched on the gravel road to our left. A lanky man with graying carroty hair sticking out from under a baseball cap stopped beside us. He held out his hand. "I'm Cal Peterson from next door. Saw your furniture van come yesterday." Cal towered over me and looked to be a good six inches taller than Ben, which made him well over six feet.

We introduced ourselves and Cal asked, "You folks work in Victoria?"

"We're retired," Ben said.

"Go on, you're way too young."

Blond, blue-eyed men are lucky; Ben looked forty-five rather than fifty-five. Aging had merely turned his hair and beard the colour of faded straw and he could outlast me at the gym without even breathing hard. Dark women aren't so lucky; my long braid of black hair was laced with silver, though Ben tried to convince me that I hadn't changed a bit since our wedding day.

"Well, I'm not really retired." Ben waved his hand at our land. "I've always wanted to have a little farm. No more rules and regulations, no more eight-to-five routine. Fresh home-grown vegetables and fruit." He looked at Cal. "Have you lived here long?"

"Born in that house right there." Cal pointed to a mossy, cedar shake roof barely visible beyond the blackberry bushes marking our northern boundary. "Anything you want to know about the island or getting things done, just ask me."

"Thanks." Ben nodded at the set of parallel iron bars set flat into the ground between our two gate posts. "Okay, first question. What are those for?"

"Cattle guard. Guess you folks don't know much about farming."

"I learn fast," Ben said. "But I never saw one of those before. How does it work?"

"See, it hurts the cow's feet, stepping half on the bars and half on the empty space between. So they stay off it. You planning on raising any cattle?"

"Maybe one cow and a calf each year for the freezer."

"We might raise cats, too," I said, tongue in cheek. "I've had some experience with that."

"We aren't going to raise cats," Ben retorted. "I know purebred kittens sell for big prices but the costs are bound to wipe out any profit."

I should have known Ben would do the research. Cost accounting was in his blood and he'd even got into the habit of applying profit principles to our private lives. His desk was always awash in detailed budgets. I was hoping retirement would cure him, because I had no intention of raising kittens to sell. If I lucked into any kittens, I intended to keep them forever.

Ben pointed to the right of our tattered house. "See the fenced area there with the little shed? Figured I'd plow it up for a garden and sell vegetables."

Cal rubbed his jaw. "That's near two acres. You'll need a better fence to keep the deer out. Anything under eight, ten feet, they'll jump it."

A rabbit popped out of the blackberry bushes hedging the west side of our land from the road. I hadn't noticed there were vines on three sides of the property; Ben's first cash crop might be blackberries. Unless I took up making blackberry wine to drown my sorrows. The rabbit stared at us in astonishment, waggled its ears and scooted away.

"Could have a problem with rabbits, too," Cal added.

"Not with a good dog around," Ben said. "I'm going to get a pup and train it. But first I want to build a carport and a workshop, fix up the chicken house."

"Our house needs fixing, too," I reminded him.

Cal removed his cap and smoothed back his hair. "The agent tell you that well's inclined to go dry in summer?"

The well was fifteen feet from the back door, on the orchard side, and the real estate blurb had referred to it as 'picturesque.' It was four feet in diameter, protected from the elements by a thigh-high stone wall and a peaked wooden roof. A wooden lid kept debris out of the water but the small oaken bucket and crude winding handle suspended beneath the roof were purely for show. The pump house, attached to the back of the house, had apparently been built for midgets. The only way Ben could get in was on his hands and knees. When, at his suggestion, I'd crawled halfway in to see what a water pump looked like, spiders and strange little black insects scuttled in every direction. I backed out too fast and banged my head on the door frame.

"The agent said it was only twenty feet deep," Ben said, "but with all the rain we get on this coast, I don't think there's much danger of it going dry."

"Uh huh." Cal reached in his shirt pocket. "Well, you want any help, let me know. I do electrical work, plumbing, carpentry, just about anything you need." He handed me a business card that said 'Mister Fix-it'. "I'll drop around again when you're settled in. Gotta go feed my Angoras."

After he strolled away, I said, "Do you suppose he has Angora cats or Angora goats?"

"Could be either. He seems like a bit of a character."

"If he meant cats, I want to see them. But I guess that can wait." I gazed at our tumbledown kingdom. "We need a name for our farm. How about Adriana Acres?"

"This country has been using metric for years. Make it Holly Hectares."

"No thanks!" I'd finished high school before the government introduced the metric system and I still hadn't got the hang of it. Mostly because I didn't want to.

"Let's finish unpacking. We can think of a name later."

"I'm going to organize my office." It was hard to believe I actually had my own space. Now, with time and country quiet, perhaps I could polish the short mystery stories I'd been scribbling for years. I'd picked the big room in the northeast corner of the house, with one window overlooking the veranda, meadow and sea and another with a view of the old orchard screening Cal's farm from our house. The scenery would keep my mind off the peeling wallpaper until we redecorated but the place stank of mouse droppings.

"I want to get a cat soon so we can put the run on those mice."

"Traps work just as well. And they'd be cheaper."

"Ben, cats have personalities the same as people and they're a lot of fun. You'll enjoy having a cat once you get to know it."

"When we get a guard dog, you can make a pet of him. I just don't see the point of having animals unless they earn their keep."

Ben's attitude was another challenge, like the house, the chicken coop and all those things Cal had said about rabbits and deer. With the right cat, though, I was sure it would be the easiest to overcome.

II - THE COMING OF THE KING

"Distinguished, dignified gentleman seeks new home with loving caretakers. Tabby-Siamese cross. Does not like other cats."

I circled the ad. Across the table, which was littered with toast crumbs, hammers and assorted bags of nails, Ben muttered over the editorial page. Since Ben always muttered over editorial pages, I had no way of telling whether he was in a receptive mood or not. He'd agreed to a cat, but he might try to delay the evil day. I crossed my fingers under the table for luck.

The cat being a loner could be a drawback but it was possible he might just need some tenderness. Or, if he had a strong need to be head cat, the assurance that he had the position permanently. Before I'd married Ben, I always had two or three cats living with me and my experience convinced me that I could eventually coax this distinguished gentleman into accepting house mates.

I took a deep breath and handed Ben the classifieds. "Let's call and find out about this little guy. He needs a home and it sounds like he's been well looked after."

Ben pushed aside the editorials with exaggerated reluctance and read the ad. "If the owner wants to put him up for adoption, why not take him to the SPCA?"

"If he isn't adopted quickly he'll be put down. There are so many abandoned animals they don't have much choice."

"I hate the idea of animals being put down." Ben frowned. "But why not settle for the dog I'm going to buy? Dogs are affectionate, loyal and bright. And they have personality."

"Cats are all those things, too."

"You have an overactive imagination."

I could deal with cats' idiosyncrasies; surely I could deal with a husband who thought they didn't have any. When I brought up the subject next day, I'd made a shopping list. Litter box, litter, wet and dry cat food, dishes, brush, catnip, toys. I handed it to Ben.

"Looks like we are about to adopt a cat. Whoopee."

He scanned the list. "Seems a sizeable capital investment for one small animal. Well, at least the cat is free."

I escaped into the hall and picked up the phone before he thought to ask how much the cat's annual shots and visits to the vet would cost. Ben was a generous soul at heart and I knew that once he'd had been won over by this dignified little gentleman, he wouldn't mind the vet bills. Provided I gave him some figures before he started drafting his next batch of budgets.

I punched the number in the ad and Karen, owner of the 'dignified gentleman,' asked, "Have you owned a cat before?"

"Several."

"Do you have any children?"

"No. Why?"

"George doesn't like them," she said. "Children are too rough and noisy."

"I have a question. Does George use a litter box?"

"Yes, but he prefers the outdoors. Do you live in a house or an apartment?"

"A house on five acres."

"That sounds very nice." I could hear new respect in her voice. Land in or around Victoria is expensive. She probably thought we were rich and would provide George with a diamond collar.

"Do you go away much?"

"Hardly ever." The cost of a workshop and double car port, not to mention house renovations, meant vacations in the Caribbean or ski trips to the Swiss Alps might have to wait for a couple of centuries.

"What part of town do you live in?"

"We don't. We live on Adriana Island."

"Oh!" I could almost hear her reassessing our probable net worth. "Is there a vet on the island?"

"Two, actually."

In the ensuing silence I pictured Karen gnawing her bottom lip and wondering if she dared trust me with her gentlemanly treasure. Finally she said, "Would you like to come and see him?"

Next day we caught the noon ferry. I ignored Ben's grumpiness and tried to subdue my own excitement, hoping the cat would cooperate, though I knew there was a chance he'd decide he didn't like us.

Sunlight danced on the waters of the Strait and the air was so warm it could have been midsummer instead of mid-March. In the cramped coffee shop on the upper deck, we found Cal Peterson nursing a coffee, his baseball cap pushed to the back of his head.

He waved us over. "Been wondering how you guys were doing. I notice you got all that junk in the yard hauled away and cut the grass. It looks a lot better."

"Thanks." Ben slid into the booth. "I'm getting more and more curious about the people who lived there before. Why would they put in that expensive swimming pool when the rest of the place needs so much work?"

"Oh, them!" Cal removed his cap to run his fingers through his thinning hair. "They were party animals."

"So that's why the hen house was full of empty beer bottles," Ben said. "I made just over thirty bucks taking them back to the liquor store."

"At least you got a little something for your trouble," Cal said. "The reason for the pool is they had a couple of young teenagers who complained there was nothing to do."

"I could have found them lots to do," Ben said. "Cal, have you got any free time? I want to get the workshop and carport built in a hurry so I can start on the garden before it's too late in the season."

Cal took a grubby notebook and the stub of a pencil from his shirt pocket and leaned forward. "Well, now, I figure we can work out something agreeable."

While the two men talked, I sat by the window and watched the bow wave ripple by, flashing in the sunlight. Mesmerized by the luxury of sitting still and doing nothing, my mind wandered to the farm. I was a little worried about the money we were putting into building and renovation but surely we'd recover that when we sold two years down the road. In the meantime, I might as well take some pleasure in living there.

I decided that what we needed was a sandstone path from the veranda to the pool. We'd put deck chairs on the wide concrete apron and it would be heaven to sit out there in summer sun, reading while Ben took a dip now and then. In August we'd be able to reach out from our chairs and pick blackberries from the thick mass of vines separating the pool from the fenced paddock where Ben planned to put the vegetable garden.

The pool would be an enticement for family to come and visit, too. Now that we had spare bedrooms instead of just a couch in the living room, I was looking forward to seeing more of Gareth and his wife, Sue. Gareth had been ten when Ben was widowed and if he'd suffered any trauma over being motherless for half his growing up years, it certainly didn't show. By the time Ben and I married, Gareth was at university but he came home often, sometimes for the whole summer, and we had a relaxed, easy relationship.

Then there was my sister, Ginna, and her husband, who might come down from Dawson Creek for summer holidays. And my Aunt Ruth from Fort St. John or Ben's family from Moose Jaw. There would be plenty of opportunities for barbecues and people splashing in the pool.

Our future dog and cat family would loll in the shade of the young alders beside the equipment shed at the end of the pool. A cold beer for Ben, a dry martini for me, catnip for the cat. And maybe a rawhide chew toy for the dog. If I could shut my mind to all the disadvantages of living on an island farm, maybe sitting beside the pool would feel like being on vacation. I must have been smiling at the thought because Ben frowned at me and said, "What?"

***

We found George in Karen's garden, picking his way on delicate paws among the tulips and daffodils and making playful passes at bumble bees. He had a short-haired dark gray tabby coat with black markings, the long, slim body, legs and tail of a Siamese and small dainty feet. One look at that aristocratic heart-shaped face, dominated by large green eyes and big ears and I fell in love.

"Why are you giving him away?" I asked. I couldn't understand her parting with such a beautiful cat. Was there something wrong with him?

Karen looked uneasy. "He gets into fights with his brother, Duffy."

Duffy, very much like George and every bit as gorgeous, came around the corner of the house and strolled sedately toward us. He sat at my feet, his trusting little face tilted up. Are you a new friend?

George vaulted a row of yellow tulips and landed beside me. Duffy retreated to a safe distance. George rubbed his cheeks against my calves, marking me as his property, and sat with his front paws raised, like a dog, begging to be noticed. I picked him up and he snuggled his head under my chin. In love for barely three minutes, now I was ready to commit myself to him for life.

"Hasn't George been neutered?" I asked.

"Yes, but he's very territorial."

At this point I didn't care whether he was territorial or not. "We'll take him."

"One last question," she said. "Do you work?"

"Not any more. Why?"

"George likes a lot of attention."

"Don't they all!" I said. "Ben, bring the cat carrier in, will you?" I couldn't wait to get this elegant feline home and make friends with him.

After George was in the carrier, I glanced up to see tears sliding down Karen's cheeks and knew she was worrying about whether she'd done the right thing.

"He'll be all right, really," I said. "Would you like me to phone and tell you how he's doing?"

She gulped, nodded and fled into the house.

During the half hour drive to the ferry terminal, George complained nonstop, his tone demanding and indignant. Clearly he was a normal cat, used to getting his own way. It was a relief to leave him in the car and escape to the upper deck for coffee and a stroll.

"I didn't know cats made so much noise," Ben said. "Is he going to keep that up?"

"Not when we let him out of the carrier. He doesn't like being locked up."

George cursed steadily for the entire five-mile drive from the ferry to our house. Ben held the carrier steady on his lap and glared at me as though the yowling were my fault. I ignored him. Ben was often snarly or gruff to hide his cream puff interior.

I released George inside the back door and showed him the litter box in the laundry room before he trotted off to investigate the house. He must have sniffed every inch of it because two hours elapsed before he returned to the kitchen and graciously accepted a meal.

At eight he announced that he'd had a very nice visit, thank you, but it was time he went home. He stood at the kitchen French doors and demanded that we open them.

"You live here now," I told him.

He glared at the door, then yelled at me. *Filthy kidnapper! Let me out!*

To escape the circular argument, we went to bed early but sleep was impossible. George paced the hall most of the night, giving vent to a penetrating Siamese yowl. At the dawn of history, similar feline howls must have made our ancestors huddle closer to the fire. Between yowls, we could hear him scratching somewhere in the kitchen.

"If he does this every night," Ben said, "one of us will have to go. And it's not going to be me."

"He's looking for his old familiar surroundings. Cats are very attached to their territories."

"Dogs get attached to people." Ben buried his head under his pillow.

Next morning, we found the bottom three feet of the white net curtains over the French doors in shreds.

Ben scowled. "Holly, look what your blasted cat's done. He's worse than useless, he's destructive."

"He didn't mean to be; he just wanted to go home. That netting was due for retirement, anyway."

"I don't care. If he scratched at the window, he'll scratch the furniture, too. If we keep him, you'll have to get his claws removed."

"Never! He's an outside cat and he needs claws to protect himself. For grooming and balance, too."

"You owe us for a set of curtains," Ben said to George, who was pacing, ears back, tail lashing in anger. And to me, "He hasn't used the litter box."

"He's fine. Cats have twenty-four hour bladders."

An hour later Ben was still fussing. "Maybe that woman lied when she said George was house-trained."

"She didn't seem to be that kind of a person. You have an overly suspicious mind." But his comment worried me.

"I don't want him to do anything on the rug," Ben said. "Maybe you should take him outside for a walk."

"I didn't buy a leash. Anyway, cats don't like being controlled. He'll use the litter box when he's ready."

Another hour passed. "I'll take him out myself," Ben said. "Can't be much different than walking a dog. I'll rig up a little string harness for him."

Protesting, George was tied into a string harness and carried outside.

Two minutes later there was a shout at the back door and I rushed to open it. Ben hurried in, holding the cat at arm's length, both of them with big, round eyes, like two startled owls. He put George on the floor and the cat bolted, trailing string, into the living room, where he disappeared behind the couch.

"He panicked," Ben said. "Sniffed the air for a minute, then took off like a streak. If I hadn't had the string wrapped around my hand he'd have been long gone. I had a hell of a time picking him up."

He undid his belt and lowered his jeans. "See what he did? I hope I don't need stitches." There were four red slashes across his thigh.

Oh, dear, I thought, this is not a good beginning.

"He was probably frightened. This is strange territory to him. I'd say he was trying to get away from you so he could go look for his home."

Ben grunted and asked if we had any peroxide. This was not the time to tell him any more of my war stories about cats; he was too busy living his own. I hoped George would do something endearing before Ben lost his temper.

I finished dabbing peroxide on the scratches, which I noted had barely broken the skin. So much for needing stitches! I wondered if Ben would charge the cost of Bandaids against George's column in the budget.

Ben pulled up his jeans. "Holly, if that cat messes on the rug, we're taking him straight back to Victoria."

George stayed behind the couch and I worried about his bowels, his bladder and Ben's edict. By noon, I'd coaxed him out and cut off his nifty string harness. By three, to my intense relief, he'd used the litter box twice.

When we settled in the living room after supper, George sat at my feet and stared into my face for a few minutes. Apparently deciding I was a reasonable substitute for Karen, he curled up on my lap and purred while I stroked his soft, silky coat and admired his tiger markings.

"Why did he pick your lap to sit on?" Ben demanded. "I'm the one who took him for a walk."

I decided not to remind Ben that cats don't like being taken for walks. "He knows I'm a Cat Person."

I wished George had sat on Ben's lap. Ben would never be able to resist that green-eyed little face purring up at him. But George was not yet ready to forgive Ben the string harness.

Ben examined the scratches on his leg and gave George a resentful glance. "I just had a thought. Why did that woman want us to take George and not Duffy?"

III - ASSUMING THE THRONE

Karen's reasons for giving us George instead of Duffy soon became obvious. George seemed to have an almost insatiable need for love and lap time; the moment I sat down he was up on my knees, wanting to cuddle. He followed me from room to room, talking and scolding, as if he couldn't bear to let me out of his sight.

"Is he going to be like this forever?" Ben grumbled.

"I'm sure it's temporary." I crossed my fingers behind my back. I'd learned from experience that cats believe they own their owners, but George was taking things to extremes and it worried me. I kept telling myself he'd settle down once he bonded with us. Meanwhile, I had to persuade Ben to go along with George's eccentricities until he fell in love with the cat himself. "Once he forgets his old territory and feels at home, he'll relax."

"I'll believe that when I see it."

George was determined to prove that the house was his kingdom and we were his servants, bound to obey his every wish. By the third day I was calling him King George the Magnificent. Ben, whose hobby was the study of ancient Rome and who liked to show off in Latin, called him Georgius Felinus Rex. His giving George a nickname seemed a good sign.

Like most cats I'd known, George was a creature of habit and demanded punctuality in his slaves. If I wasn't out of bed when the sun lit the eastern horizon, George reminded me of my duties by yowling in my ear. If that didn't work, he'd try to dig me out from under the blankets or tickle my face with his whiskers and purr loudly. Cats are stubborn, but I'd never met one this persistent. No matter how many times I threw him off the bed, he was back in ten seconds, intent on getting me vertical.

"Why don't you put him in the hall and shut the door?" Ben asked.

"Once I'm on my feet and walking, I'll be wide awake. Which means I'd never get back to sleep so I might as well stay up. George will still get what he wants."

I didn't mind too much because Ben and I had agreed sleeping in could wait until we had the buildings and garden shipshape. Still, six o'clock did seem a trifle early.

"Just ignore him," Ben murmured. "Maybe he'll get tired of nagging and go away."

Before I could think of a reply less profane than the one on the tip of my tongue, Ben drifted off again. The man could sleep through anything, including a radio blasting the morning news into his ear. Even more annoying was the fact that George nagged me, the understanding, helpful Cat Person, but never Ben, the one who really needed training.

A few days after George arrived, we shifted our bed and dressers to one of the three attic bedrooms in preparation for the eventual renovation of the main floor. The King's efficiency as an alarm clock soon proved to be considerably less than that of the bird population.

Starlings had found a way into the enclosed storage space under the roof slope and built nests there. The nestlings rose even earlier than George and woke us at first light, yelling for worms until the alarm shrilled at seven and startled them into silence. The parent birds gave them morning running lessons, too, and it sounded like each baby starling weighed at least fifty pounds. The thunder of tiny feet and the anguished squawks when they apparently fell over something we'd thoughtlessly left in their way guaranteed that we were awake long before we wanted to be.

"As soon as those babies leave the nest," Ben growled, "I'm going to starling-proof the eaves so tightly not even a fly will get in."

George was neither disconcerted by the new locale for our bedroom nor distracted by birds he couldn't see. He resorted to new tactics to get me out of bed. He threw things off my dresser. He scratched his head with his hind leg, causing his ID tag to rattle noisily. Finally he stretched up full length, extended all eighty claws, and ripped the wall beside the bed.

Though the wallpaper was old, stained and due to be replaced eventually, this was too much for Ben. "That cat is not going to tear the house apart whenever he feels like it. You'll have to do something."

For a week I kept a plant sprayer full of water beside the bed and used it on George every time he scratched. The sprayer was discarded the night when, half asleep, I held the thing the wrong way round and sprayed myself so copiously I had to dry my hair and change my pajamas.

Ben stopped laughing long enough to say, "I thought you were going to clip his nails."

"I will. First thing tomorrow morning." I'd been putting it off on the pretext that I was too busy but, in fact, I hated the job. It was all too easy for me to walk a mile in George's paws, and the thought of someone forcing me to sit still while she cut my fingernails was repugnant.

"Good! Then we can sleep a little longer."

"How? Our starlings scream at dawn, roosters crow next door and Cal hammers nails at eight in the morning."

"Gotta get the workshop built fast so I can get started on the garden."

The voice of sweet reason rolled over and went to sleep. I lay there indulging in nostalgia over our condo in Victoria, so well insulated we couldn't even hear the woman next door play her violin. Sure I liked animals, but did they have to talk so loudly? Where was all the country peace and quiet I'd been told so much about?

Next morning I carried the nail clippers and George to the couch. We snuggled and purred at each other until he was half asleep. By the time I'd finished his right front foot, he was struggling, but I persisted. When the left foot was done, he flounced away, stopping once to give me a look that said he'd sell me back to the slave dealer if I tried that nonsense again.

Later I sat bleary-eyed in my studio, snatching a couple of hours at the computer to start a new short story instead of running errands for Ben and Cal. As I stared at the monitor, a traitorous thought occurred to me. Would Karen agree to swap Duffy for George? Immediately a wave of guilt swept through me. How could I even think of giving up a cat as affectionate as George? Besides, we belonged to each other now. Feeling sentimental, I typed 'mother and son.' Then deleted it. Tyrant and slave was more like it. I headed for the phone.

Karen recognized my voice as soon as I said her name. "You're not bringing George back, are you?"

"No, but I would like to know why you gave us George instead of Duffy."

She sighed. "George is very aggressive and demanding. Duffy isn't. They're the first cats I've ever had and I just thought George needed someone who'd know how to deal with him. I sure don't."

"Have you had them since they were kittens? I'd like to learn something about George's history."

"No," Karen said, "only about six months. But I have Marilyn's phone number. I got the cats from her."

Marilyn sounded curt and distracted at first but thawed when I told her what I wanted to know. "Those cats haven't had an easy life. Duffy's all right, he rolls with the punches, but George has a different personality. I wanted to keep them but my mother had a stroke and I've got all I can do to look after her."

I sympathized and she went on. "For one thing, the kittens were taken from their mother far too early. Duffy may have looked on George as his security blanket but George didn't reciprocate. Then the first owners abandoned them when they were six months old. They spent several weeks on the street, starving."

Poor little George! It was heartrending to think of him thin and hungry, his lustrous fur dull, seeking warmth and food and love and having every door shut in his face. When I was six, my parents had accidentally left me at a campsite because they were in hurry to get my sister and her broken arm to a hospital. They were back in minutes but at the time those minutes seemed like years. "So George became aggressive and attention-seeking because he was insecure?"

"I think so," Marilyn said. "They'd been in eight different homes by the time I got them, which didn't help."

"No wonder George is insecure. Cats need to have a permanent territory. How old is he? Karen wasn't sure."

Marilyn thought for a moment. "About five, I think. Are you planning to keep him?"

"Definitely. Now that I know why he's so possessive perhaps I can convince him that I'm his forever."

"I doubt if he'll get over all his bad habits," Marilyn said, "but one can always hope."

She wished me luck. I hung up and said to George, who was batting at the telephone cord, "We have two hurdles to overcome, Your Majesty. You have to trust me to take care of you forever and we both have to convince your other slave that you're worth at least ten dogs."

He nuzzled at my chin and purred. I decided to regard that as a good omen.

***

After about ten days, when I was sure the King had bonded to us and his new territory, I let him out. Green eyes wide and nose questing the air, he crept belly down across the front veranda. Then under the veranda. Ben hovered in the background, asking, "Where is he now?" every thirty seconds or so. I couldn't tell whether Ben was concerned about the cat getting lost or hoping he would.

I called to George to reassure him that his head slave was at his beck and call. He floated onto the veranda and turned to gaze at the sloping meadow and trees which separated our farm from the beach properties below.

Does all this belong to me, too?

I told him it did. Tail high, he trotted down the steps, turned left and raced through the orchard into the thick blackberry vines that separated Cal's land from ours.

"Doesn't he have sense enough to stay in his own yard? Cal's goats will eat him." Ben didn't sound particularly sorry about the prospect.

"He'll come back," I said, secretly worried that he wouldn't. "He's just exploring."

We waited ten minutes. George did not reappear.

"I suppose I'll have to go look for him," Ben said. "The stupid animal is probably disoriented and confused." He disappeared down the road, calling, "George! George!"

I decided to join the hunt myself and started by calling George from the veranda. He bounded out of the brush, galloped across the yard and joined me.

"Good boy! This is where you live, remember?"

He butted my hand with his head and trotted off to examine the meadow, stopping to sniff every second blade of grass. I got on with making lunch.

Twenty minutes later Ben returned. "I can't find him anywhere. He must be lost."

I led him to the veranda and pointed.

"I suppose he was here the whole time I was walking up and down the road yelling my head off. The neighbours must think I'm crazy."

"I doubt it. George probably does, though."

George was delighted with his territory and spent much of his time exploring it. Since he wanted to make short but frequent forays, we spent much of our time letting him out and letting him in.

"This is ridiculous," I said. "Let's put a cat flap in the back door."

"I agree," Ben said. "Why should we have to open doors for him twenty times a day?"

"He's been waking me up almost every night for butler service, too. I'd be much happier if he opened his own doors. I don't like stumbling up and down those stairs at two in the morning."

"He thinks it's your duty," Ben said. "But it isn't fair that His Majesty should be forced to go to the trouble and effort of rousing us."

"Rousing me, you mean. You sleep through all of it."

Ben and Cal took time off from the workshop project to install a cat door, only to discover that George thought it beneath his dignity. Why should he push that silly flap with his head when he owned two perfectly good servants? I tried coaxing. I tried swearing. I tried tuna.

Nothing worked. George stalked away every time and I resigned myself to door duty.

A couple of mornings later, I let George out of the kitchen French doors and started washing dishes. Suddenly he was sitting at my feet.

"How did you get in?"

He kneaded the linoleum and stared at me with wide, innocent green eyes.

When Ben and Cal came in for lunch, I said, "George finally used the cat door on his own."

"I'm glad he caught on," Ben said. "Now you won't have to go crashing down the stairs to let him out and I can get a good night's sleep for a change."

"That cat's living in clover with a door all his own," Cal said, dunking a cookie in his coffee. "Daisy stays outside all night." Daisy was Cal's cat. I'd seen this multi-coloured fluff ball from a distance but hadn't yet managed to make friends. "My girlfriend, Sylvia, has two cats and they stay out overnight, too."

I was surprised to learn Cal had a girlfriend. He'd never mentioned a wife and we assumed he was the crusty old bachelor type.

"Where does Sylvia live?" I asked, ignoring Ben's frown. He thought I was prying. I was. But only because I liked Cal.

"Ellis Bay." This was a settlement of some two dozen houses at the southern end of Adriana, a distance of thirty miles of rutted gravel road.

Before I could ask Cal why he and his lady didn't move in together, Ben finished his coffee, stood up, and said, "Well, let's get back on the job." Cal grabbed another cookie and followed him.

As it turned out, Ben was wrong about George accepting the cat door. His Majesty proceeded to instruct us on protocol. A royal personage has the right to be waited on. Otherwise, what's the use of being royal? He ignored the cat flap during the day and demanded butler service at the French doors, the front door to the veranda or the back door. In, out; out, in; and if we didn't obey instantly, he yowled his displeasure at the top of his semi-Siamese lungs. I could and did ignore him much of the time but Ben leapt up the moment George yelled. After one particularly busy evening, Ben said grimly, "I'm going to design a family crest for that cat with the motto Vexo."

"Vexo? What does that mean?"

"It's a Latin verb meaning 'I pester'."

"I've told you why he pesters. He'll get over it when he feels more secure."

"I know he had a rough time in the past, but like Cal said, George is living in clover now."

"He isn't sure it will last. And he doesn't understand that you can't stand the sound of a cat crying."

Ben snorted. "He can cry all he wants. I don't care."

That didn't fool me for a minute. I was amused by the 'vexo' label, though.

Next morning, I saw George creeping up on a squirrel. "Come back here, Imperial Vexator!" I realized at once this was too big a mouthful to scream across the yard. And, not only did George ignore me, but the mailman, shoving mail into our box from his open car window, looked at me as if his doubts about my sanity had been confirmed.

It wasn't long before the Imperial Vexator struck again. When Ben and Cal came in for coffee, Cal said, "Don't suppose you could keep that cat in during the day, could you? Every time I climb up the ladder, he climbs up after me and then he won't move when I want to come down."

***

George continued training us. When he tired of being petted, he'd pick up my hand with his sharp little teeth, gently but firmly, and put it away from him. If I persisted in reading when he wanted petting, he nibbled my fingers, just hard enough to imply that if I went on ignoring him I might end up like shredded tuna.

Ben and I learned that if we did the same thing at the same time three days running, it became, for George, an unbreakable tradition. He had a remarkable sense of time and we found ourselves retiring to bed with books and cups of tea at ten p.m. because George started herding us in that direction at nine fifty-five. Once there, he snuggled up for long sessions of petting and purring. When we turned the lights off, he slept curled around the top of my head, lecturing me if I moved. I sometimes woke to find him stretched across my throat, blissfully asleep. Much as I enjoyed having a warm, soft cat to sleep with, I wished he would spend more time lying on the bed than on me.

One evening I was alone. Ben had gone to Victoria on business and I didn't expect him back until the last ferry so I watched a movie that ran until midnight. George paced, his tail a flag of disapproval. He spoke to me sharply. He sat on the coffee table and nibbled my bare toes. For two hours he did everything he could to make me shut off the television but I held out. It was a good movie.

At midnight I plugged in the kettle and went upstairs to change into pyjamas. George raced ahead and sat on the bed to supervise. When I headed for the door, he tried to stop me by hooking his claws into my dressing gown.

"George, I'm only going to fetch the tea."

As I reached the bedroom door, two furry legs gripped my ankle and sharp teeth nipped it. Startled, I dislodged him and took two more steps. This time the other ankle got it. Apprehensive now, I picked him up at arm's length, lugged him downstairs and put him outside to cool off.

When he came back in, through the cat door for a change, he was gracious and charming, apparently writing off my revolt as a temporary aberration. I never knew for sure; the tea-making and my leap into bed had been at top speed, achieved before his return.

But George had another grievance. He did not approve of Ben's absence and told me so repeatedly while I drank tea. He continued to complain until Ben arrived at one a.m., then paced back and forth, lecturing, while Ben undressed and got into bed.

"What's the matter with him?" Ben asked.

"He missed you." This was a blatant lie. Actually, George was annoyed because his male slave hadn't come to bed at the proper time but, if Ben thought George was fond of him, he might be won over.

Ben gave George an appraising glance, said, "Hmph," and fell asleep at once. I lay awake trying to think of more ways to prove to Ben that George liked him.

Next day, Ben and I were both exhausted. George was as energetic and urbane as ever.

A week later we returned from a movie in Mora Bay to find His Majesty pacing at the bedroom door with a look of grim anticipation, ears back and that black and brown striped tail lashing from side to side. I flipped on the bedroom light.

The Royal Avenger had pooped on Ben's pillow.

Ben looked shocked, then angry. "Why would he do such a thing? You said cats were fastidious."

Through my laughter I managed to gasp, "What on earth did you do to him?"

Defensively, "I didn't do anything."

"You must have," I said. "Using your pillow as a toilet is a statement that he's really mad at you."

"Are you sure? Do cats actually do that?"

"I'm positive. Look at him; he's waiting for you to figure it out and apologize."

While he cleaned up the mess and changed the pillow slip, grumbling to himself, Ben tried to think what sins he'd committed against cathood.

"I think I know what it was," he said. "I unwrapped a new shirt this morning and snapped it hard to get out some of the stiffness. George was right at my feet. He jumped as though he'd been shot and ran out of the bedroom."

"He believes you did it on purpose. Cats hate loud, sudden noises."

Ben looked thoughtfully at George, who was now trying to round us up and put us to bed. "I'm ready to capitulate on two points. One, George is very intelligent. Two, cats do have personalities and this one has entirely too much."

Next morning Ben brought a load of clean laundry upstairs and dumped it on the bed. He picked up a pillow case to snap the wrinkles out of it, then noticed George watching him from the doorway.

Ben spread the pillow case on the bed and smoothed the wrinkles out of it with his hands. "All right, George, I give in. I am your slave, the lowest of the low, a mere insignificant houseboy."

George soared onto the bed, stretched out on the pillow case and gazed up at Ben, who hesitated, then petted George's head. The King purred and rolled on his back, letting Ben rub his tummy. From the sappy look on Ben's face, I knew my worries about him wanting to send George back to Karen were over. The King had finally succeeded in transforming Ben into a devoted houseboy and, if George was as clever as I thought, Ben would be a loyal slave forever.

IV - THE ROYAL MOUTH

Three weeks after George came to live with us, I took him to the new veterinarian in Mora Bay. George hadn't had shots during his time with Karen and I wasn't about to risk losing my precious King to rabies, distemper or feline leukemia. The April sunshine was mellow and the air fresh, but George took no notice. The yells of rage from the cat carrier kept me company all the way to town. I tried to soothe him by talking, but for all the good that did, I might as well have saved my breath.

Jerry Parker was tall and slim with brown curly hair. Cal had said he was young and would be up to date on animal medicine, but I didn't expect someone who looked as if he'd graduated from high school only yesterday.

"Well, who do we have here?" he said, lifting George from the carrier.

"George the Magnificent, monarch of all he surveys."

"I can see he's part Siamese," Jerry said. "Naturally he thinks he's royalty."

George suffered the examination and shots with bad grace and, when Jerry and I let go of him, leapt off the table and tried to crawl behind the fridge. I grabbed him and put him in the carrier, where he was so happy to be in a familiar spot, even a hateful one, that he settled down and actually kept quiet.

"He seems in fine shape," Jerry said. "Have you been having any problems with him?"

I related George's history and mentioned that the Royal mouth was not only talkative and fussy about what it ate, but also had the habit of vomiting frequently.

"He might be looking for attention. Some cats will do that." Jerry asked me several questions about George's diet, then shook his head. "I wouldn't worry about it. Cats aren't like humans; they vomit as quickly and easily as they use the litter box."

Jerry finished his paperwork. "Are you a long-time resident?"

"No, we moved here from Victoria a few weeks ago."

"Beautiful island, isn't it? Cindy and I came here a year ago because it seemed like a safe place to bring up kids. Ours are ten and twelve now." Obviously Jerry had been out of high school for several years.

"Ben and I are supposed to be retired, but we're working harder than ever, trying to develop a market garden over on Macklin Road." I was tempted to tell him that I hoped it would fail so I could go back to city life, but refrained in case he was offended. Besides, I didn't really want the garden to fail because that would hurt Ben. It would be enough, when the time came, if I simply said I couldn't stand island life.

"Have you met many of the locals yet?" Jerry asked.

"No. Just our eccentric next-door neighbour."

"A lot of those around." Jerry grinned. "One great thing about the island is that people accept you for what you are. Nobody cares if you're unconventional."

"I've heard that eccentrics tend to gravitate to islands. I'm sure some people would consider us eccentric because we're living on a small island with one movie theatre and no Cablevision." I couldn't resist a final shot. "And I'm not so sure they wouldn't be right."

Jerry lugged the cat carrier to the door. "Tell me, are you conventional enough to play bridge?"

"Absolutely!" The possibility of a bridge game brightened my day. "Do you and Cindy play?"

"We love the game but so far we haven't found another couple to make up a foursome."

"Well, count me in as a single if you want to get a game together. Ben doesn't play, unfortunately."

"I'll find a fourth," he promised.

I dropped my latest short story in the mail box, crossing my fingers for luck. I'd spent far more time on it than any of the others; surely this time I'd score. When I pulled into our driveway, George was still grousing in the carrier. "Shut up, my lord, your castle is at hand."

I released him in the kitchen and he scooted into the living room and hid behind the couch. I put the carrier away, worried that he might be so upset about his visit to the vet that he'd never forgive me.

Twenty minutes later he was winding himself around my ankles, purring. I picked him up and settled on the couch for a snuggling session. "See, George? You've still got your home and me. Every now and then we'll have to go see the vet, but I'll always bring you back again."

I thought about the people who'd abandoned him and wished I could wring their necks. A stray kitten with no mother to teach it how to hunt is almost always doomed. George and Duffy had been lucky to survive.

I bent my head toward him and he butted my forehead with his and licked the end of my nose.

The ornamental cherry trees were shedding their blooms in pale pink drifts on the grass when Ben and Cal finished the carport and workshop. Ben had tilled the two acres – or, as he called it, point eight of a hectare – in the paddock and fixed up the hen house. Our miniature farm was beginning to look respectable though I complained that the vehicles lived in a better house than I did.

"We can work on the house come fall," Ben said. "I need to do the outside work while the weather is good. The most important thing is to get that garden growing."

George the Magnificent was still working hard on getting butler service at all three doors, his successes usually due to the Houseboy being unable to ignore his pathetic wailing. Though irritated by our slowness and stupidity, George refused to give up.

He'd lead us to the door he'd chosen. When we opened it, he'd have a leisurely wash before strolling out, no doubt trying to look his best for his subjects, whoever they were. If it was raining, he scolded me for turning off the sun and sat, nose outside sniffing the air, rear end inside on a warm carpet, wondering whether to trust his precious body to the dampness. If the rain was too heavy, he headed for his litter box in the combination laundry and mud room. If not, he went out, gingerly stepping around puddles on those long, elegant black-striped legs and shaking rain drops off his royal robes. When he returned from inspecting his kingdom, he'd gaze at the landscape for a moment or two before condescending to enter, giving his invisible subjects a chance for one last adoring look.

After days of being housebound by heavy rain, Ben said, "We have to find another way for George to go in and out. He doesn't like the cat door." Now a devoted houseboy, Ben was learning to understand cat language.

Ben created the perfect access for a persnickety king. He opened the sliding window in the downstairs master bedroom one cat width and built a small wooden platform to put across the sill, just the right size for George to sit on. We put an easy chair below the sill and a block of wood outside on the ground as a convenient step. George was pleased and immediately began using it as a throne where he could sit and survey both his inside and outside kingdoms by merely turning his head.

I was not pleased. In the next hour, I spent as much time capturing the winged wildlife that came in through the open window as I would have letting George in and out. By suppertime, I'd put glass tumblers and thin pieces of cardboard in every room for the capture and release of wasps and bumblebees. George took care of the grasshoppers and spiders himself, crunching these disgusting morsels between his teeth with as much enthusiasm as Ben ate salted peanuts.

However, when I discovered that George took care of moths, my annoyance changed to such gratitude that I would happily have been doorman for the rest of his reign. Fluttering moths sent me into mindless panic and George, shown a moth, stalked it relentlessly. He never missed. Unfortunately, they were crunchy, too.

When the rain quit, Ben said, "I'm going to Ellis Bay to pick up some chickens. Cal put me onto these people who said they'd sell some. Want to come?"

Ellis Bay was reachable by some thirty miles of cow trail that passed for a gravelled road. Ben had traded in his car for the typical Adriana pickup; old, battered and springless, though reputed to have an engine that would last for centuries. I had no wish to subject my body to an hour of Blue Betsy bouncing through potholes. "No thanks. I'll stay here and mull over my future role as Egg Lady."

Ben roared through the gate in his battered blue chariot and I went back to worrying about what to give the King for his dinner. The word 'finicky' didn't begin to describe the high standards held by the Royal Mouth. The Houseboy's mantra, repeated at least once a day, was "Please be patient, my lord. The Concorde bringing your fresh lobster from Paris is a little late today."

George was an enthusiastic diner, provided the food happened to be what he felt like eating at that precise moment. If it wasn't, he'd look at me as though I'd given him poison and try to bury the meal in the floor. If I'd wiped his place mat and scrubbed his food dish to sparkling cleanliness, opened a fresh can of Fluffytail's Incredible Edibles, and crooned to him while spooning it out, I couldn't help feeling hurt when he treated it like something he'd done in the litter box.

Nor was it enough to serve food he liked. The dish had to be clean and if the food had been there more than thirty seconds, it was stale and therefore inedible. A lot of food was sent back to the kitchen.

The week before, we'd spent half an hour in front of the cat food shelf in the Mora Bay supermarket.

"Do you think he'd like this one?" Ben asked, handing me a can.

I read the ingredients in Kitty's Divine Gourmet Sea Feast. "Sounds okay. Let's give it a try."

A voice behind me said, "Cats don't need all that fancy stuff." It was Cal Peterson, a pitying look on his face.

"Daisy catches birds and mice and only comes for dry kibbles a couple of times a day." He pushed his baseball cap back on his head and grinned. "You folks ought to get some goats. They'll eat anything."

I was irritated by Cal's smug expression and wondered if his goats had ever considered eating him. His straggly hair and the grin were probably indigestible, though.

At home, I opened the can, ladled food into the Royal Dish and George ate with gusto. Wonderful, he loved the stuff! The next week I bought a whole case of it.

Now I opened the fourth expensive tin of Kitty's Divine Gourmet Sea Feast and spooned it into a clean dish. George took one sniff and walked away, ears laid back, a moué of disgust on his face.

How dare she feed me that garbage!

I picked him up and put him in front of his dish several times but he stalked away. After Ben left to get the chickens, I gave up. Poor old suffering George would have to starve.

"I don't feel a bit sorry for you. Pat and prod and meow all you like, but I am not opening a different brand of food just to keep you happy. Go out and catch a mouse."

He flicked his tail and raced through the house, up the stairs, and back down, doing his Siamese war cry. When he stopped at my feet, I was ready for him with a length of string. Our favourite game was for me to pull the string along the floor so he could pounce on it. It was certainly more fun than trying to feed him.

***

A couple of hours later, Betsy roared into the yard and backed toward the hen house. From beneath an orange plastic tarp covering the pickup box came loud, indignant squawking.

I went out, George trotting at my heels. "Are they in there loose?"

"Didn't seem worth the trouble to build crates." Ben untied one corner of the tarp. "Now, you hold the tarp down so they don't get out. I'll reach in and grab them one at a time and put them in the hen house."

Ben stuck his hands into the box, yelped and jumped back. Startled, I let the tarp go slack and a pure white Leghorn rooster with a great plumed curving tail and murder in his eye squeezed out and hit the ground running. He headed straight for George.

After a split second of wide-eyed shock, George streaked for the back door, the rooster within inches of his tail, and dove through the cat flap, which swung back and smacked the rooster in the beak.

I couldn't help laughing. "Finally! A surefire way of getting George to use the cat door."

The rooster turned and came at me. I let go the tarp and ran to the other side of the pickup. At once a flurry of white and rusty-red hens scrambled out of the box and flapped in all directions, squawking hysterically. The rooster lost interest in me and started rounding them up.

Ben alternately sucked his bleeding finger and swore. "Now they'll be all over the country. Why did you let go of the tarp? The rooster wouldn't have hurt you."

"Oh, really? Then why are you bleeding?" He had sense enough not to answer that.

"I got a dozen white Leghorns and a dozen Rhode Island Reds, plus Mister High and Mighty there." By this time Mr. Mighty had subdued most of his flock. "Looks like he's good for something besides keeping George humble." Ben headed for the small shed beside the chicken house. "I'll put food and water inside so they'll know where to roost tonight."

"I've got some scraps for them." When I came out carrying a tin of Kitty's Divine Gourmet Sea Feast, Ben looked astonished.

"You're not going to give them that, are you? It costs an arm and a leg."

"I'm going to feed it to somebody," I said in a firm voice. "If you don't want to volunteer, it'll put some meat on Mr. Mighty's bones."

"Just leave the stuff in George's dish. When he gets hungry enough, he'll eat it."

"Sure, and those hens are going to lay golden eggs."

***

"I'm making beef stew with red wine for tonight," I said, when Ben came in later.

"George won't like it; he hates onions."

"We don't have to feed him at the dinner table."

"Is there any ham?" Ben asked. "He likes that."

"I ate it for lunch."

"Cruel! Thoughtless!" Ben teased. "Well, I guess poor George is going to be stuck with cat food."

At dinner, George got canned tuna fish and ate it from a dish beside Ben's chair. Or rather, he took each piece out of the dish and put it on the rug before eating it. But how could a mere slave complain? Besides, I had no one who would listen. Ben had gone from 'cats are boring' to

'George is wonderful' overnight. He'd become so enamoured I worried that my efforts to train George would be cancelled out by Ben's efforts to spoil him rotten.

The Houseboy suffered guilt pangs while he ate his beef stew. "I know the service is bad around here," he said to George. "I'll make you some chicken tomorrow."

"If you let him out, he can go to the hen house and catch his own dinner."

Ben shook his head. "George will never get any fresh chicken with Mr. Mighty on guard duty."

I didn't think we would, either.

A few moments later Ben said, "The Frasers have a Samoyed bitch. She's due to pup the end of May."

"The people next door to my Dad's farm had a Samoyed. They're beautiful dogs. Are you going to get one?"

"I think so. They're working dogs; they were used to herd reindeer and haul sleds. Should be easy to train a pup to keep deer out of the garden."

"Sounds fine to me. I wonder what George will think."

"Oh," said Ben, "don't worry about George. The dog will keep him in line, no problem." A pause. "Maybe George is eccentric enough to eat dog food. It would be a lot cheaper than what we're feeding him."

"Don't change your budget in anticipation of a miracle like that. Our hens really will lay golden eggs before George lowers himself so far as to eat dog food."

V - GLORY OF THE CHASE

One bright Friday morning in late May I woke up without the help of George's usual meowing in my ear. Wondering where my fur-covered alarm clock had gone, I sat up and swung my feet over the side of the bed. One foot touched a body that was too warm to be a rug and couldn't be George because it didn't yell with indignation. I yanked my feet back under the covers and peered over at something that looked very much like a giant mouse. I poked Ben.

"I think there's a dead rat on my rug."

Ben struggled out of bed, fumbled for his glasses and came around to my side. He looked at the large gray-brown shape on the bedside mat.

"Yes, that's a rat. Don't move; I'll get rid of it." He went downstairs and returned with a brown paper bag for the corpse. "I wonder when George brought that in."

"I'm just grateful he didn't put it on the bed or lay it out artistically on my chest."

"That cat still owes us for a set of curtains, too."

He took the paper bag outside to the garbage can.

Hunting has always been popular with kings and George was determined to be in the royal swim. Now that he had a handy window portal, he was showing off his championship style. In the last three weeks he'd presented trophies to us almost every day, his tail waving high in triumph.

"If George were a dog," said Ben, "these kills would be gifts to the head dog, namely me."

"But George is a cat and a king. He's simply showing his humble subjects that he has superior hunting prowess."

George did nothing so crass as to eat his trophies. After all, when one has an imperial residence and slaves and is accustomed to Fancy Feast on a gold plate, one does not eat raw bird or mouse. One merely drops them, still bleeding, sometimes still running or flying or crawling, on the living room carpet and awaits, with regal dignity, the adulation due a mighty hunter.

"Why does he insist on bringing his catch into the house?" Ben asked.

"I read somewhere that cats bring prey to their humans because they think we're large, stupid kittens and they're trying to teach us how to hunt."

Ben snorted. "George isn't teaching us how to hunt. He's never had any doubt that we're too slow and stupid to catch anything."

The week before, we'd started a new game: tossing ping pong balls at George. He obligingly batted them back to us but we always missed. I had to agree that George knew we could never catch a mouse. Bringing his trophies into the house was just his way of bragging.

"George," I said as I put down his breakfast, "don't show off with any more rats. Please? And eat your food or I'll give it to Mr. Mighty and the hens. They're not picky."

He sniffed the food and decided it was edible. Peace reigned.

After lunch, Ben said, "Why don't we try out the pool later this afternoon? It's warm enough now."

"You try it out. I'll relax in a deck chair with a martini and we'll pretend we live like rich folk all the time."

Ben went off to weed the garden and fiddle with complicated pool mechanisms. I gave myself an hour in my studio to mull over a poem I'd written about peaceful sunlit May mornings. I'd barely reread the draft when George bounded into the room with grasshopper legs sticking out one side of his mouth.

"Oh, George, not again!"

He released the grasshopper, which ricocheted off the walls, the furniture and me, with George in avid pursuit. The grasshopper finally leapt across my desk toward the window sill, George two leaps behind. Papers, books and pens skidded to the floor.

I'd learned to move fast in order to rescue George's live prey but I could not catch grasshoppers. Nor did I want to stay and listen to the crunching while he ate one. I left, shutting hunter and prey in my studio.

I went back fifteen minutes later but the grasshopper had vanished and George's face wore a smug expression. The studio looked as if a tornado had been through it. I tidied up, no longer in the mood for literary pursuits, and spent the next couple of hours cleaning house and baking cookies. Ben's son, Gareth, and his wife, Sue, were due to arrive next day to celebrate Ben's birthday and have their first look at our mini-farm. When Ben came in at four, I was more than ready for a break.

The pool was too small for swimming lengths but Ben splashed and paddled and dove, pretending he was an otter. George paced around the concrete apron, meowing, while I sipped my martini and enjoyed the sunshine. He seemed relieved when Ben climbed out, opened a beer and flopped in the deck chair beside me.

The Houseboy gave George a doubtful glance. "I wonder how he's going to react to Beanbag." Gareth had mentioned on the phone that he and Sue had adopted an adult Welsh corgi and that the dog weighed over forty pounds.

"I'm worried about how Beanbag is going to react to George. A ten-pound cat is no match for a heavy dog."

Sometime after midnight I wandered down to the kitchen to get a glass of milk, not bothering to turn the light on, as I like to wander around in the dark and am blessed with good night vision. An odd shape lay beside George's food dish. I bent for a closer look, then went back up to bed and poked the Houseboy.

"There's a rabbit beside George's food dish."

"Don't be silly," he said groggily. "You must have been dreaming."

"No, I wasn't."

He climbed out of bed and into his glasses and, to my annoyance, turned on the bedside lamp before departing for the kitchen. A few minutes later he was back.

"You're right. It was a rabbit."

"Is it dead?"

"Yes. I put it in the garbage."

George's prey was getting bigger and bigger. Maybe the corgi wouldn't be a problem after all.

***

Gareth and Sue arrived on the ten o'clock ferry next morning and found their way along the winding gravel road to our retreat. Sue unfolded her tall, slim body from the car and rushed into my arms for a hug.

"I brought you a jade plant," she said, pushing her long blonde hair back over her shoulder. "Nobody can kill a jade plant." All my plant-loving friends thought they could cure my brown thumb.

Gareth, who had grown a short beard that matched his father's, gave my braid a gentle tug and told me I looked younger than ever. "Country life must agree with you."

"I'm surviving, at least."

He took Beanbag out of the car and snapped on his leash. "Better safe than sorry; I have no idea how he reacts to cats."

We went in the back door, Beanbag straining ahead on his leash. George, who had been asleep on the couch, came trotting into the kitchen to see what we were doing. At the sight of Beanbag, his green eyes got big, his back arched and his tail fluffed to twice its size. Crouching in attack position, he hissed and growled ferociously.

"I'd better shut him in my studio," I said.

I needn't have worried. Beanbag whimpered and scuttled behind Gareth's legs.

"Look at that!" Gareth unsnapped the corgi's leash. "We've obviously got ourselves one big wuss of a dog."

Beanbag backed into a corner, still whimpering. George edged closer and hissed again, but Beanbag merely cowered. George's back and tail returned to normal and he sat down within a few feet of the corgi, eyeing him warily.

"I wonder why he's afraid of cats," Sue said. "Most dogs like to chase them."

"Ask his former owners," I said. "I'd like to know the secret of George's power over him."

After a quick tour of the house we went outside to show off Ben's new workshop and the pool. Sue was much more interested in our ocean view. She asked, "Is there a path down to the beach, or do you have to go around by the road to get there?"

"We've got a path," Ben said. "Why don't we take a walk down there now?"

"Wait till I grab my sketchbook." Sue ran to the car.

"I'll get Beanbag," Gareth said.

"Put him on the leash. I wouldn't want George chasing him up a tree," I teased.

"George doesn't go for walks, does he?" Sue asked.

"Of course he does. He goes everywhere we go."

We strolled down across the meadow, Beanbag practically clinging to Gareth's ankles and George, still cautious, keeping a prudent distance. The walk was easy now that Ben had cleared a path through the maples, cedar and arbutus at the bottom of our land. I pinched a frond of cedar needles and inhaled the delicious pungent scent. The salal rustled as George raced through it, chasing imaginary elephants. He seemed like a wild creature out here and I had a quick flash of wonder at his willingness to share his life with me.

When we reached the fence and the road beyond it, Gareth said, "I thought your land went right to the beach."

"If we win the lottery, it will." Ben spread two strands of barbed wire so Sue and I could climb through. "Those lots across the road are quite small but one of them would cost twice as much as we paid for our two hectares."

"Five acres," I said.

"Well, nobody makes waterfront any more," Gareth said.

We groaned at the cliché and straggled across the road and down the public access to a little bay with a pebble beach. The sun was warm and tiny wavelets lapped softly at the gravel. Gareth and I sat on a driftwood log and talked technology – he was a computer technician for a logging company in Campbell River – while Sue sketched the bay. Ben had taken over protecting Beanbag from evil cats and he and the dog patrolled the outgoing tide, looking for crabs. George swished through long grass on the bank, no doubt looking for more grasshoppers to give me.

"Oh, that was heavenly," Sue said an hour later, as we wandered back across the road, heading home. "Do you spend much time down there?"

"Not as much as I'd like to," I said. "Looking after chickens, a big garden and a falling-down house takes a lot of time. Not to mention a demanding cat."

"Come on, you're maligning that poor innocent little creature." Sue reached down to pet him but he eluded her and raced into the trees.

As we reached the meadow, George came out of the bush behind us, a small bird clamped in his jaws, and streaked for the house.

He was waiting for us in the living room, the bird still in his mouth.

"George, let it go," I said in my sharpest 'rescue' voice, grabbing him around the middle. He opened his mouth and the bird flew into the window, nearly knocking itself out. George kicked me in the stomach and tried to take off after the bird.

By the time I came back from locking him in my room, Ben had caught the bird and let it go outside.

"Does George catch many birds?" Sue asked.

"Yes," Ben said, "but we manage to release most of them unharmed. If their missing feathers grow back and they don't end up having heart attacks next time a cat comes along, they probably live to a ripe old age."

"I didn't notice any bird feeders," Gareth said. "You built bird feeders for me when I was little, remember?"

"I'm not wasting feed on wild birds that can look after themselves," Ben said. "Besides, they don't do anything useful and George would just catch more of them."

I took pity on George, yowling in the studio, and let him out. He raced back to the living room and sniffed at the few feathers his bird had lost while Beanbag, whining, tried to squeeze himself under Ben's recliner. George paced, complaining loudly that we couldn't even catch a bird when he'd trapped it inside the house for us.

"He doesn't bother showing us how to catch mice any more," I said. "He just leaves dead bodies on the floor."

"He's very good at catching rats and mice," Ben said. "I'm the one who has to get rid of them, though; Holly can't bear touching dead animals."

"Ben spoils him with so much food I'm surprised he bothers to hunt. But hunting is an instinct and he'd do it no matter how much food he was given."

"He's just proving to Dad that he's useful," Gareth said, winking at me.

***

After a trip to Mora Bay to explore a couple of small craft galleries, the others had a quick swim and then joined me for a cocktail beside the pool. A cool breeze came up and sent us inside for a second drink and plates of crackers and provolone cheese.

His Royal Highness could scent cheese the way Ben could scent trouble in a new government budget and he was soon on my lap, trying to get at the piece I had hidden in my hand. I popped it into my mouth. He stood up on his hind legs and gently patted my lips with one paw.

"Look at him!" Sue poked Gareth in the ribs. "I'd never have believed that if I hadn't seen it."

I put George on the floor and crumbled some cheese for him. Soon we moved into the dining room for Ben's birthday dinner of baked chicken. This was George's favourite meal and he wanted it handed to him bite by bite off the Houseboy's dinner plate. Ben rationed it carefully, afraid George would eat too much and upchuck.

When George had had six or seven small bites, Ben said, "That's all there is, George."

The King knew that was a bald-faced lie. He paced around the Houseboy's chair, complaining. Ben gave him a small piece of broccoli.

George bit into it, spat it out and marched away, ears back and tail quivering with indignation.

"I feel terrible doing that to him," the Houseboy said.

"Would you prefer scrubbing the carpet?"

Ben's face cleared and he tucked into what was left of his chicken, with a couple of muttered remarks about dogs he had known and how easy they were to feed.

After dinner, the four of us sprawled around the living room, gossiping, while Beanbag slept under the coffee table.

"Have you thought of a name for the farm yet?" Gareth asked."

"Yes," I said, "Holly's Folly."

"You don't mean that," Ben said, a hopeful expression on his face. "You love it here."

"You wish."

Ben sighed.

A stealthy movement caught my attention. George, belly to the floor, was creeping up on the dog.

Corgis may not stand tall or look graceful but they are hunting dogs, very fast. Beanbag seemed to fear cats, but I didn't trust his reaction to claws waking him out of a sound sleep. I grabbed His Magnificence just as he was about to launch himself, removed him to the safety of my studio and shut the door.

"What was that all about?" Sue asked.

"George thought he was going to have Beanbag for a midnight snack."

"That cat is crazy."

"Not so loud!" I warned. "He's into big game hunting now. If he hears you bad-mouthing him, you could be next."

"I think you should call the farm 'Animal Crackers'."

"We're the ones who are crazy," Ben said. "George knows exactly what he's doing."

When Gareth and Sue headed upstairs to their bedroom, I said, "If you use the bathroom during the night, leave the door open when you come out. George's drinking water is in there."

"Why?"

"His Highness is as finicky about where he drinks water as he is about what kind of food he'll eat."

Drinking water had never been a problem with other cats I'd known. Water is water is water, as Gertrude Stein might have said. But not to George. His water dish, cleaned and refilled daily, sat next to the waste paper basket in the bathroom because he simply would not drink out of it anywhere else.

"We'll take Beanbag in our room, just in case your mad king decides to attack him again," Gareth said.

About three a.m. I made a trip to the bathroom, blinking in the bright moonlight that bathed the hallway. There sat George, head forward, ears perked. Two feet from him was a garter snake, coiled upward in rattler fashion, staring back at him. In spite of my large size and clumsy feet, neither paid me any attention.

I could think of only one solution. I tiptoed down to the kitchen, got a heavy saucepan lid, brought it back upstairs, and placed it over the snake. Then I went to the bathroom. When I got back into bed, I poked the Houseboy.

"There's a snake in the hall."

VI - BIG GAME HUNTING

"That rooster woke me up at five this morning," Gareth complained, as he and Sue joined Ben and me at the kitchen table. "I thought country living was supposed to be peaceful and serene."

"That's what Ben said when he was trying to talk me into moving here," I said.

"Mr. Mighty wants everyone to get up and admire the new day. And himself, of course." Ben poured the coffee, smiling and no doubt congratulating himself on his agility in changing subjects.

"George is a night bird, too." Sue rubbed her thigh. "When I went to the bathroom at two this morning, he pushed the door open and came in for some water. Then he jumped on my lap and kneaded my bare thighs. My skin feels like a lace table cloth."

Gareth smiled. "When I went in, George sat and stared at me the whole time. It was almost embarrassing."

The phone rang and I handed Ben the spatula. "The bacon's almost ready to come out. And one of these days we have to get a phone in the kitchen."

I came back from the hall, elated, and said to Gareth and Sue, "That was my sister, Ginna, in Dawson Creek." I turned to Ben. "Tom's been transferred to Calgary and they're getting a month's holiday before they go. They want to come and spend it with us."

"What will they do here for a whole month?" Ben asked.

"Tom loves building things." I stirred sugar into my coffee. "He says he wants to help renovate the downstairs."

"I think it's a great idea," Gareth said. "Maybe I can come over for a couple of weekends and help out, too."

"I'd be crazy to say no." Ben gave me the spatula. "Bring on breakfast, Holly, we have to build some muscle."

A surprised and strangled "Caw!" sounded from the veranda.

A crow. Even with a quiet morning and the front door open, it sounded much closer than usual.

Another "Caw!" from the living room.

Ben and I raced for the doorway and collided as we tried to get through it at the same time.

There was George the Magnificent, lean and mean, his teeth clamped on the neck of a crow as big as himself, dragging the bird across the floor to his killing ground behind the couch.

Ben yelled and George let go of the crow. The terrified bird flapped around the living room, defecating with every wing stroke. George raced back and forth below and Beanbag stood in the doorway, barking furiously.

We used a broom to chase the crow out the front door, George running after it and cursing us for losing yet another of his trophies.

"If this was ancient Rome," Ben said, "the senators would grant George a triumph."

"What does that mean?" Sue asked.

"George would wear a special purple toga and parade around the yard in a chariot with the crow in chains walking behind him." Ben nodded at me. "His head slave would walk beside him, holding a laurel wreath over his head and reminding him every so often that he's mortal, like everyone else, therefore he shouldn't get a big head."

I reached for the rug cleaner. "I remind him every day that he's merely a cat with too much attitude, but it doesn't do any good."

After breakfast, Ben opened the French doors and looked out. "There's not a crow in sight. If we taught George to catch one every day, that might keep them away permanently."

"You must believe in miracles," Gareth said. "Besides, I don't think you're teaching George anything; he's teaching you."

Ben frowned, remembering all the things George had taught him. "But we could encourage him. Then, if we kept the doors shut and blocked the cat flap, he couldn't bring them in."

"I bet you believe in the tooth fairy, too," I said, patting his arm.

***

After Gareth, Sue and Beanbag left, taking with them three dozen large brown eggs, I said, "It's time I started my career as an egg lady; the fridge is still full of eggs." I didn't expect it to be demanding; we were on a back road and most of the customers would be neighbours.

Ben went out to nail a sign on the gate post saying we had eggs for sale and I went to tidy the living room. George lay sprawled in a patch of sunshine, green eyes glinting under half-shut lids, whiskers white against his dark fur. He looked so relaxed I wished I could trade lives with him for awhile. A cat sunning himself, utterly abandoned to the sensual joy of warm sunshine, is the best demonstration of how to live each moment to the fullest, an art form in itself.

When Ben came in, George had twisted himself into a black-striped pretzel to bathe a hind leg. When that was finished, he unwound himself, licked a paw and wiped his face with it.

"Look at him," Ben said. "He's actually washing his face like a human being."

"Don't say that! He'd be very insulted to be compared to a lowly human."

"Have you noticed he licks his paw on the average of four times before wiping his face once?" Ben watched George wash the other hind leg and resume bathing his face. "He licked his paw only once that time and wiped his face four times." It was not the first time I'd noticed that cost accountants like counting things.

"A choreographer could create an interesting dance sequence from his washing routine," I said. George ignored our rude personal comments and continued his graceful ballet solo. Finally he stretched out, rolled on his back and gazed at the ceiling.

"Contemplating the mysteries of life," Ben said.

"I wish he'd spend more time doing that. He's clever and funny but sometimes he makes life so interesting that I yearn for a little boredom. I wonder if he's ready to accept a second cat."

Ben looked doubtful. "He was ready to attack Beanbag. I think he'd give another cat a rough time."

"Maybe he does need more time to realize he has a permanent home with us. But I want another cat, so he'll have to get used to the idea sometime."

"We don't need two. George does a fine job of catching rats and mice. Anyway, he's special. You'd never find another one with a personality like that."

Suddenly George sat up and cocked his head.

"What do you hear?" I asked. He leapt to the back of the couch and looked toward the garden. Ben went to the window.

"Deer!" He dashed out the front door, leapt over the veranda railing and ran toward the garden. He flapped his arms at the deer, but was within six feet of them before they moved and within three before they reluctantly jumped the fence and ambled down the slope into the trees.

Ben came back red-faced and furious. "I'm going to phone Cal Peterson. Maybe he knows a way of getting rid of those corn stealers without building a ten-foot fence."

"You should have taken George out there. He'd have bagged one all by himself."

"Don't be funny," Ben snapped. When he came back from phoning, he said, "Cal says we should put urine in tin cans and place them every few feet along the fence."

"Why would that work?"

"He didn't know, he just said it might. Or we can tie lengths of our hair to the fenceposts."

"I wasn't planning to have a haircut any time soon. And you don't have enough to even think about it." Ben had spent ten years in the military during his first marriage and still favoured very short hair.

"Well, I'm going to try the urine. Don't flatten any more tin cans for the recycle box, okay? And how about potting those cherry tomatoes I bought yesterday?"

"Why don't you put them in the garden?"

"The plants and pots and soil cost me over twenty dollars; I'm not letting the deer eat them."

"Ben, you know they'll die if I touch them. Remember what happened when I tried to grow some on the condo balcony?"

"You can't possibly ruin cherry tomatoes." His faith was touching, if misguided.

I spent a half hour filling pots with black soil and crooning over the plants to make up for my ineptness. The veranda seemed a good place for them; they'd get plenty of sunlight, yet be protected by the house.

Later that night, after wondering aloud if George would ever catch another crow, the Houseboy said, "I suppose he's like Tiberius and Nero. He's become bored with the mundane – now he demands the exotic."

We resumed watching television and were soon engrossed in the last five minutes of a particularly suspenseful murder mystery. I was aware of George walking purposefully along the hall past the doorway, tail carried high, but he was almost into my studio before I realized he was carrying something large and furry in his mouth.

The Houseboy went in pursuit. With a last yearning glance at the mystery, which was at the point where the Inspector gathers the suspects in the drawing room, lights his pipe and says, 'Now all shall be revealed!', I followed Ben and reached the hall in time to see George drop the body of a rabbit on the carpet. The body came to life and fled back down the hall into the master bedroom, George hot on his tail, the Houseboy hot on George's and me lagging behind. The rabbit went under the desk. George tried to follow but Ben grabbed his tail and I wondered if any of them would notice if I quietly went back to watch television.

With a great scuffling of claws, the rabbit leapt on George's chair, across his throne and out the window. The Houseboy had managed to grab more of George's anatomy than just his tail and the King was swearing in Siamese. I closed the bedroom window to give the rabbit a chance and rushed back to the living room just in time to see the credits roll by.

"George," I said, when he came back, still struggling in Ben's arms, "your timing is lousy. Next time, wait for a commercial break before you bag an elephant."

VII - UNCAGED COUSINS

Ginna called me again from Dawson Creek. "Tom's gone to Calgary to rent a house for us and driving to Victoria from there. I'd like to find a way of coming south that doesn't involve changing planes and lugging two cats in and out of taxis. Any suggestions?"

"I'll come and get you." Aunt Ruth, who lived in Fort St. John, might have driven Ginna and the cats down but she'd gone to Europe for a month. Anyway, I enjoyed driving and I hadn't seen the north country for a long time. Also, my short story had come back with a rejection slip attached to it and I wanted a break from trying to figure out where to send it next. And maybe a day or two alone in the car would provide me inspiration for a new story. "But will Clyde and Jeremy be okay travelling by car?"

"Of course. You worry too much."

"I guess they're all grown up now." I peeled George off my shoulder. His Royal Highness didn't approve of me talking on the phone when I could be more usefully employed paying attention to him.

"Clyde's turned into a master hunter," Ginna said, "but Jeremy's a lap cat."

"Do you think they'll get along with George? He's very territorial."

"If they don't, we'll have to keep them separated."

After hanging up I started worrying about leaving George alone with Ben. The King had progressed to sleeping on the bed more than he did on me and splitting his time between Ben's lap and mine. If I deserted him, would it bring back all his insecurities?

The prospect of escaping from the farm and routine for three or four days was too tempting. "He won't be any problem," I said to Ben. "All you have to do is feed and water him. And keep him out of trouble."

"What do you mean, that's all?" Ben combed his beard with his fingers and eyed the King, who was still toying with the phone cord. "While you're away, I'll make him a scratching post with a little house on top. I've got some old carpet stowed away in the work shop."

"Good idea."

"He deserves some luxuries. I haven't seen a mouse in here since he arrived."

I refrained from reminding him that he'd once thought traps were a better solution and went to pack a bag. I'd be taking the Chevy sedan, leaving Ben stuck with bouncing Blue Betsy for four days but he didn't mind; he'd even bought a straw hat to wear when he was driving her. Next thing he'd be wearing overalls and sporting a red bandana.

I set off in glorious sunshine, excited about being on the road, though it took four hours and two ferry crossings before I got to a road that actually went somewhere.

The drive through the Fraser Valley was delightful; dairy cows grazed on green meadows and the smell of fresh cut hay filled my nostrils. The Fraser canyon, which I had never driven before, sliced dramatically through steep fir-clad mountains, its wild beauty very different from the Valley. The Cariboo, its rolling brown hills dotted with sagebrush and ponderosa pine, was different again. I was in a mellow mood when I arrived in Dawson Creek.

Ginna met me in the driveway and we hugged. "What have you done to your hair? I love it." Her hair was as black as it had been when she was a girl and cut short to swirl around her neck in a pageboy cut.

Her hazel eyes twinkled. "I dyed it to cover up the gray. Besides, I was tired of wearing it long like yours."

"You look great. Are you still running five miles every day?"

"I don't have a perfect record," Ginna said, "not with the icy roads we got here last winter." She led me into the living room. "I'll order a pizza. We can eat that with our fingers. All our possessions have gone in the moving truck except for some of my clothes and the two sleeping bags we'll use tonight."

After the pizza, we settled in for the rest of the evening to catch up on the news and family gossip.

"Are you getting reconciled to farm life?" Ginna asked, when we finally headed for bed.

"It's not as bad as I thought, but I do miss Victoria. And my friends. In spite of my job, I loved the life I lived there."

"Well, wait and see," said my sister. "Nothing is forever."

Next morning we loaded the car. "Where are the cat carriers?" I asked.

"I don't have any."

"How do you get them to the vet?"

She looked at me as if I were crazy. "I carry them in my arms."

"Don't they try to run away?"

"Not so far."

I was envious. Why was Ginna blessed with such docile felines when every cat I'd ever had would disappear for a week at the slightest hint of being put in a cat carrier or car or taken to the vet? Then I was besieged with a new worry. How on earth would Ben manage if George became ill?

"They'll freak out if they're loose in the car, Ginna."

"No, they won't. They like car rides."

I didn't want to argue, but I knew that as soon as we were in the car and I started the engine, two whirlwinds of screaming fur would be rebounding off every surface.

Now the cats had disappeared. "They must know we're planning something evil for them," I said. We found them sunning themselves on the porch roof, quite unconcerned. "Okay, how do we get them down?"

"No problem. We go upstairs and I climb out on the roof and hand them in to you."

Soon the four of us were tucked cosily into the car. Slim, long-legged Jeremy, with gray fur so thick and soft that Ginna called him her velour cat, lolled on her lap. Clyde, with long white fluffy fur on belly and chest and a mixture of brown, black and orange on the rest of him, sat on the back seat.

I rubbed a hand across my forehead. "You going to behave yourselves, boys?"

"I forgot you didn't know. They're not boys, they're girls," Ginna said.

"Then why did you name them Clyde and Jeremy?"

"We thought they were male when we got them. By the time we found out they weren't, the names had stuck. And we've never been able to get out of the habit of referring to them as 'he' and 'him'."

"If they're neutered, I guess it doesn't matter."

Ginna smiled. "They are. Anyway, they don't care what we call them."

I started the car and braced myself for an explosion.

Nothing happened.

While I backed out of the driveway, my three passengers calmly observed the scenery. I shook my head and aimed the car south. I didn't mind being wrong, but nothing in my life thus far had prepared me for angelic cats.

The miles rolled by and the angels got restless. They explored the back seat and the floor where their dishes were, but refused to touch food and drink that vibrated. They meandered to the back window, then returned to the front seat to complain gently about the boring environment. Ginna was kept busy removing first one, then the other, from under my feet, off my lap, my head, or the steering wheel.

At seven that evening, we quit. I didn't want to drive one more inch and Ginna was sick of prying cats off the brake pedal. I pulled into a motel with a vacancy sign.

"I'll register," she said. "Hang on to the cats."

I got a firm grip on them and Ginna was out and had the door shut before the cats wriggled out of my hands. Five minutes later she was back, tapping on the window. I rolled it down two inches.

"There's a sign saying they don't allow pets."

I groaned.

"It's okay. I didn't tell them we had any. We're registered, but we'll have to smuggle the babies in."

"And smuggle them back in the morning."

"What for?" Ginna said. "It'll be too late for the manager to kick us out then."

I eased the car into our parking slot. "Now what?" The cats tried to crawl out through the two-inch gap above the window.

"I'll open the unit door. Then you hold Clyde and Jeremy so I can get back in the car and grab one of them. You'll have to hold the other one while I get out again."

This was accomplished with less fuss than I'd expected, but I noticed she'd left the motel door open when she came back for the second cat. "You didn't shut the door! Jeremy will get out."

"You worry too much. I locked him in the bathroom."

Ginna took Clyde and I hurried in with the cats' food, water dish and litter box. The cats strolled around as if they owned the place and seemed quite contented.

When we returned from dinner, the cats were still being angels. They snuggled on Ginna's bed while I lay awake until very late, worrying about my own demon feline and imagining in horrific detail all the major disasters that might greet me when I got home.

Next morning we put the cats and their paraphernalia back into the car. "How do we get in without letting them get out?" I asked.

"Stand on the driver's side and scratch at the window. They'll come to see what you want," Ginna said.

To my surprise it worked. Both cats stood on my seat with their angelic little paws on the window and Ginna slid in and shut the door. Then she held them while I got in.

"Hey, we're getting good at this."

Ginna smiled. "I told you it would be easy."

Two hundred miles later we stopped for lunch and did it again. I thought the cats would catch on, but they came to the window, convinced I had treats for them. I felt guilty for fooling them and wondered if they were stupid. George would never have fallen for that trick more than once.

In early afternoon we drove into the Fraser Canyon. On the way north, I'd driven on the inside lane, against the mountain. Now we were on the outside where the sheer walls of the canyon, hardly a car width away, dropped to the river thousands of feet below. I'd forgotten about my old fear of heights, now returning as full-fledged terror.

I clung to the steering wheel, palms sweating, trying not to look at the steep drop on my right. But my gaze was drawn back again and again, and each time I could feel the car beginning to move toward the edge. Heavy traffic, mostly freight trucks, roared beside and behind us, horns blaring as I lost speed. All I wanted to do was stop the car, get out, lie down and cling to solid pavement.

"What's wrong?" Ginna asked.

"I'm scared." A blast of air from a passing semi made the car shudder. "We're going to go over the edge into the canyon; I know it."

"No, we're not. There's lots of room on the road. Do you want me to drive?"

"There's no place to stop. Besides, I can't keep the cats away from you if I'm lying on the floor with my eyes shut tight."

"I don't remember you being afraid of heights when we were kids," she said.

"I was too ashamed to admit it." Ginna, a year younger than me, had been a fearless tomboy. "Talk to me. Tell me stories. Keep me distracted."

"What kind of stories?"

"Anything! I don't care. Something bizarre. Or funny. Tell me about your sex life. Just get my mind off this horrible canyon."

I've never found it easy to tell stories on demand, but Ginna came through as if she'd trained for it. She told me tales about the cats, then every dirty joke she'd ever heard, and those got me through the next mile, and the next, and the next, and finally out of the canyon. I pulled off the road onto a side street in the first small town and sagged against the backrest.

"We're almost there," Ginna said. "Another hundred miles to the Tsawwassen ferry and then another few miles to the Adriana ferry and we'll be home."

I lit a cigarette and realized my hands weren't shaking any more. "You're right. Nothing to it." I rolled my window down to suck in a big breath of fresh air.

Something landed on my shoulder and the next thing I knew, Jeremy was out the window and streaking toward a small yellow house with flower baskets hanging at the corners.

"Oh, Ginna, I'm so sorry!" I hurriedly rolled the window up before Clyde could follow. "I'm such an idiot." I felt like crying; my thoughtlessness had lost Ginna her special velour cat.

"Grab Clyde," she said, getting out of the car. "I'll go look for Jeremy."

I stroked Clyde and bit my lip to hold the tears back. If she couldn't find Jeremy I'd never be able to make it up to her. But she'd barely reached the end of the driveway when he trotted down it with a pink fuchsia in his mouth and dropped it at her feet. She picked up cat and fuchsia and strolled back to the car. I held Clyde while they got in.

"Good boy," she said to Jeremy. "You always bring me flowers, don't you?"

"You're joking."

Ginna laughed. "No, I'm not. He used to sit for hours under our hanging baskets in Dawson Creek, waiting for flowers to drop, then pounce on them and bring them to me."

"Maybe he could teach George to bring me flowers instead of rats and rabbits."

We made the three o'clock ferry, leapt out of the car and locked our two frustrated and now vociferous passengers inside. For the next hour and a half we walked on deck, admiring the ocean and catching up on more family gossip. I was so relieved that the Fraser canyon was behind us and both cats were in the car that I didn't worry about one single solitary thing.

As the ferry nosed into the dock, we returned to the crowded car deck and I reached in my bag for the car keys.

They weren't there.

I searched frantically through my pockets. Not there, either.

"Ginna, did I give you the car keys?"

"No."

"Now what will we do? I've lost them."

She peered into the car. "They're in the ignition."

We stared at each other. The windows were shut except for the driver's side, which I'd left open an inch so the cats could get air. All around us car engines were being revved by drivers anxious to get off the ferry and hit the road again. Our line of cars began to move and the ones behind us honked angrily. The cats, looking frightened, were pacing restlessly inside the car. I thought they must be as terrified of the noise as I had been of the canyon.

"Do you think, in the next five seconds, we could teach Jeremy to pull out the keys and hand them to me through the window?" I asked.

"He's not that wonderful." Ginna went in search of a crew member to rescue us.

Five minutes later a deck hand unlocked the door with the help of a coat hanger. "Good thing you left that window cracked," he said. "These Chevys are hell to break into."

Once more we went through our ritual of climbing into the car without letting the cats out and were waved off the ferry by impatient crew members.

A mile down the road, Ginna said, "You feel like stopping for coffee?"

I moaned.

"You worry too much," she said. "You always did. I was only kidding."

When Ginna and I walked in the back door, Ben took one look at me and stuck a stiff scotch in my hand. I collapsed on the couch while Ginna shut her two babies in my studio.

"Rough trip?" He mixed a gin and tonic for Ginna.

"Let me put it this way." I took a bracing sip of scotch. "Clyde and Jeremy were unbelievably well-behaved. But I'll never take another cat anywhere, ever, unless he's in a cat carrier."

"Never mind," Ben said, "George missed you as much as I did. All he's done for four days is follow me around, demanding to know where I hid your body."

"Is that really all he did?" I asked, remembering the awful things I thought he might have done.

"He threw up on the bed once," Ben admitted. "He was asleep on it when the urge hit him. He didn't do it because I was mean to him." He caught my expression. "And, yes, I did wash the bedspread."

"Where is he?"

"The last time I saw him, he was sitting on the fence teasing Cal's goats."

The cat door slammed and George raced into the living room. After so much concern about my absence, did His Majesty greet his head slave? Of course not.

He turned his back and sat in the doorway, pointedly ignoring me. When he decided I'd been punished enough for leaving him, he wandered over and sniffed my ankles. Scenting Clyde and Jeremy, he turned his back on me again and walked away, tail flicking.

"I guess he thinks I've been unfaithful."

"He's more concerned that you went missing for four days. Slaves are valuable property, you know. In ancient Rome, they were sometimes branded on the face to discourage them from running away."

"I'll stay out of range of his claws for a while then. Did you make a scratching post?"

Ben nodded. "It's in the workshop. I thought you could give it to him as a present to make up for having left him all alone for four days."

"He wasn't alone. He had you."

"Tell him that."

Ben had become a true cat lover. When I got another cat I'd have far more trouble with George than with Ben. Two cats, or half a dozen, would be no problem when we moved back to Victoria at the end of two years. My Aunt Peggy's house was roomy and so was her yard. My only problem at the moment was to convince George that we needed another cat.

George returned ten minutes later, leapt onto my lap, purred, and nuzzled my chin lovingly. I was so glad he'd forgiven me for deserting him that I didn't even care about the cat hair in my scotch.

***

"Shall we introduce the cats?" Ginna put down her empty glass.

"Now? I don't know if I'm ready for this."

"It'll be all right. Clyde and Jeremy are easy-going and they know they're in George's territory. George can't fight if nobody will fight with him."

George prowled back and forth in the hall, the tip of his tail wig-wagging his displeasure about the two felines he could smell. Ginna opened my studio door.

Jeremy was sprawled in a pool of sunshine on the floor. Clyde perched on the corner of my desk. For a moment George stared at them, then dropped to his belly, laid his ears back and inched toward Jeremy, his growl rising to almost a scream as he threatened murder.

"Now we're for it!" I said.

Jeremy yawned and lazily rolled onto his back, waggling his front paws and exposing his soft, vulnerable tummy. George stopped moving. After a moment he marched over to Jeremy and smacked him on the nose. Jeremy hissed but remained supine.

"I told you it would be okay," said Ginna.

George, having beaten Jeremy into submission, decided to deal with Clyde. He jumped onto the desk and crouched in battle mode, growling again. Clyde hunched, growling back. George snarled and spat, smashing Clyde across the face. After a tense moment, Clyde carefully backed away, inch by slow inch, until he could leap to the window sill.

George's tail was lashing. I was afraid he'd chase Clyde and continue his attack, but he jumped down, strolled regally into the hall and disappeared. Clyde and Jeremy relaxed and went back to sprawling.

"There," Ginna said. "That was easy, wasn't it?"

"Ginna, maybe I do worry too much. But somebody has to do it."

VIII - REVAMP CAMP

Ginna's husband, Tom, arrived a few days later. As he got out of his van, I noticed he'd given up on his thinning hair and shaved it off.

"The polished head looks good," I said, hugging him.

He grinned. "No combs, no brushes, no shampoo. I always did like the simple life." He was shaking hands with Ben when he saw the well. "Is that for real?"

"As real as it gets," Ben said.

"No kidding!" Tom took the lid off and peered into the depths. "I thought it was some kind of fancy decoration."

"The pump house is beside the wood shed." Ben pointed at the two structures attached to the back of the house. "I don't think you'll fit through the door, though." Tom was a big man with broad shoulders that had served him well when he played football in college.

He opened the door, bent down and peered at the pump. "Interesting." He backed away and looked at the pump house itself. "Wouldn't take much to enlarge that."

"Holly wants her house fixed," Ginna said.

Tom laughed and hugged her again. "No kidding! Let's get at it, Ben. Pour me a beer and we'll walk around the inside and see what needs to be done."

I had visions of the entire house being gutted by six in the morning and Ben and Tom hard at work with hammer and saw. For one insane moment, I thought of rushing inside and making a dozen casseroles in case the stove disappeared.

Ginna looked at my face and said, "Relax! They won't start tonight. Not if I have anything to say about it."

***

At six next morning the house was still peaceful, except for the unmistakable sound of George upchucking. I wondered whether he was doing it because of Clyde's and Jeremy's invasion of his kingdom or my desertion of him for four days. Or just because he felt like it.

I heaved my protesting body out of bed, put on my dressing gown and found my glasses. I usually rose an hour before everyone else so I could ease into the day before life slammed me in the solar plexus with some new problem, but now George had ruined my treasured hour of quiet.

His Magnificence often ate grass as a pre-breakfast hors d'oeuvre and I knew this was a Good Thing because it cleansed his system. But why did he then gallop into the house and throw up his grass plus all the water he'd drunk in the last twelve hours onto the living room carpet?

Downstairs, I got some paper towels, trying to be thankful for the small pleasures of life, such as the prospect of breakfast. Then found cloths and the rug cleaner. By the time I'd mopped, sprayed, scrubbed and dried George's target area in front of the couch, I was feeling less than benevolent toward the feline species. George watched all this activity with bright-eyed interest, waiting to see what strange thing I'd do next.

"Why can't you be helpful like Burma?" I growled at him. Burma was a sleek, black cat who lived with my friend Barbara in Victoria and helped her with the housework by dragging paper towel and toilet rolls from the basement storage room up the stairs to the front hall. In honour of his work, Barbara had renamed him Sherpa.

George, predictably, ignored my question and demanded food. I was up, wasn't I? That meant it was breakfast time, didn't it? I washed a cat dish, opened a can of food and placed breakfast in front of His Majesty. He devoured it with every sign of enjoyment and I was just beginning to relax and anticipate my first cup of coffee when I heard gagging.

George had upchucked his entire breakfast on the living room carpet. Not on the kitchen linoleum, which would have been easy to clean, not outside, where I could have ignored it, but on the living room carpet. In a different location from his first creation, naturally.

By the time I'd cleaned it up, George was announcing that he was ravenous and wanted something decent to eat, not that garbage I'd tried to foist on him earlier.

"You can starve to death for all I care," I told him. "That was a perfectly good breakfast and you've always liked Fluffytail's Gourmet Crab Tails and Shrimp Heads. You threw up on purpose, I know you did."

George refused to confess to anything so gauche and continued to nag. I finally gave in and opened a can of PurryPuss Venison. I knew from experience that he wouldn't eat Fluffytail's Gourmet Crab Tails and Shrimp Heads again that day because it was the awfulness of that putrid offering that made him throw up in the first place.

His Magnificence ate and I followed him around for ten minutes, prepared to heave him out the nearest window if he hunched into spewing mode. When he went outside, I relaxed with my toast and the crossword puzzle.

Ben appeared at seven. "You're up early."

"I awoke to rosy-fingered dawn painting the sky in hues of peach and gold and was moved to leap from my bed with a song in my heart and a smile on my lips."

"George threw up again, huh?"

Some time passed in healing silence, Ben engrossed with the editorial page and me with my crossword. George raced into the house, the cat flap swinging wildly in his wake, and one second later came sounds of hacking and coughing and heaving from the living room.

The Houseboy hurried in to assess the situation.

"George just threw up a hair ball and what looks like most of his breakfast," he reported.

"That's nice, dear," I said. "The rug cleaner is under the sink."

***

When Tom, Ginna and their two cats came downstairs, George hissed at Clyde and Jeremy, who hissed back. I was starting to panic when Jeremy flopped on his back, showing complete submission. It was poor old Clyde who got smacked in the head again. George sat down for a thorough wash, then demanded we open the back door for him. He paraded out as though he had important business on his mind. Clyde and Jeremy rubbed around Ginna's ankles, looking for breakfast.

Over his second coffee, Tom said, "Let's move everything out of Holly's studio, the bathroom, the master bedroom and Ben's den and do the whole north side of the main floor at once."

"Okay," Ben said, "then we can move everything from the south side over and do the living and dining rooms, the kitchen and the laundry room."

Ginna rose. "Let's get at it, guys. My specialty is stripping wallpaper."

"Should we block the cat door so Clyde and Jeremy can't get out?" I asked.

Ginna said, "You worry too much. They know home is where I am, so they won't go far."

Ben gave Ginna's cats a wistful glance. "They haven't caught any mice yet but they're well-behaved. They haven't thrown up once since they got here."

We moved furniture into the living room until it looked like a crowded secondhand store. I shuddered at the disarray and hoped nothing essential was buried under it. Ben said, "Don't hide Georgius Felinus Rex's scratching post behind all that stuff; he won't be able to find it."

When Ginna finished laughing at George's elegant Latin title, she said, "He'll find it. Cats have a much better sense of smell than humans."

"Maybe so, but it's not fair to confuse him by shifting everything around." Ben insisted on putting the scratching post in the hall, where George would have immediate access and the rest of us could trip over it. There was no doubt George had the Houseboy completely under his paw.

We moved boxes of books and linen upstairs. Ben, Tom and Ginna stripped wallpaper, ripped up linoleum and dismantled the bathroom. I made grocery lists, did two loads of laundry, watered the garden and gathered the eggs, barely escaping with my life when Mr. Mighty chased me out of the hen house.

I was putting trays of eggs in the fridge when there was a rap at the back door and Cal Peterson walked in.

"Morning, Holly. I need a couple dozen eggs."

"You're my first customer! I'll celebrate by giving you an extra dozen free to mark my debut as Egg Lady." Getting rid of three dozen meant more space in the fridge for the mounds of groceries I needed to buy.

"Who belongs to the Ford Bronco in the driveway?"

"My sister and her husband are here for a month to help renovate the house. Why don't you see what they're up to? Ben mentioned getting you to do some electrical work."

Cal disappeared down the hall and I drove into Mora Bay to pick up groceries and supplies for the renovation crew. When I got back it was time for lunch, then more errands and prepping supper.

By five o'clock everybody was more than ready for a swim and a drink. "Ah, this is heaven," Tom sighed, climbing out of the pool and flopping into his deck chair. He took a gulp of cold beer. "Country peace and quiet, clean air, green growing things, no traffic."

Clyde and Jeremy, lying under Ginna's chair, yawned and blinked as though in agreement. George sat on the diving board, looking down on the other two cats through slitted green eyes. I'd just concluded that he was working out some fiendish plot to push them into the pool when I heard footsteps and the tinkling of a bell.

I turned to look and nearly dropped my martini. The yard was full of Holstein cows, black and white hides like checker boards melting in the sun, munching grass and leaving an occasional contribution of fertilizer.

"Those are Ken Dyckman's cattle," Ben said. "Hey! Get out of here!"

Two cows lowered their heads and eyed him suspiciously; the rest ignored him and went on eating. While the cats retreated to the safety of the blackberry hedge, the swimmers, barefoot and still dripping water, harried the dozen cows back across the so-called cattle guard and down the road with me trailing along in the rear.

Halfway to Ken's place, we met him, tramping along in rubber boots and carrying a pitchfork. "Sorry about that," he said. "Had a guy with a backhoe doing some ditching and he busted the fence. Got it fixed okay now."

"Want help getting them back in the field?" Tom asked. I could see that Ginna's city boy thought chasing cows was a big adventure.

Ken shook his head. "No, Marla's waiting at our gate. We'll get them in okay. Thanks anyway."

We strolled home and Ben sank into his deck chair. "What was that you said about peace and quiet, Tom? And no traffic?"

***

I soon learned that renovating required endless decisions. There seemed to be thousands of paint colours to choose from in the hardware store. And should we use oil-based or water-based? Should we put in new double-glazed windows or leave that for later? What kind of carpet? What colour? What type of baseboard? Should the oak flooring in the hall be replaced? Or sanded and refinished? Ben spent every lunchtime studying his cost estimates and cursing contractors and inflation.

"Come on, Ben, it's not as if we can't afford it." We were barely halfway through the nice little chunk of money Ben had inherited from his father two years before.

"It's the principle of the thing!" He caught my expression and smiled sheepishly. "Well, these estimates were accurate three months ago." He shook his head. "Just the same, if prices keep going up, we really will be broke by the time we're through the reno."

I left him to his favourite hobby and made coffee.

As if the decorating decisions weren't enough, I also had to decide what to feed four people — five when Cal was there — and three cats. Three times a day. I was now well acquainted with the clerks at the hardware store and lumber yard. If I didn't appear at least once a day, they said they missed me. I'd even learned to drive bouncing Blue Betsy with some skill, though little enjoyment.

By the time two weeks had passed, the north side of the house was finished, right down to the books being back on the bookshelves in my den. Clyde had claimed my big chair for sun-filled afternoon naps. Jeremy had discovered the rose bush by the veranda and frequently came trotting in with a yellow rose petal in his mouth for Ginna. Ben and I moved back downstairs to the master bedroom. George paced around the house, sniffing each new change and, with due ceremony, was dubbed Royal Building Inspector.

Ben and Tom were moving living and dining room furniture to the veranda and covering it with a tarp when there was a knock at the back door. It was the plumber I'd been nagging for days by phone.

"Mr. Jeffs, I'm delighted to see you!"

He looked surprised at the warmth of my reception. "Guess you must be in a hurry to get that bathroom done."

Since we'd been waiting for him for two weeks I doubted 'hurry' was a regular part of his vocabulary, but at least he knew what it meant. I didn't tell him Ben and I had been so eager to move back to our downstairs bedroom that we'd forgotten the main floor bathroom was out of commission and were developing thigh muscles and great lung capacity tramping up and down the stairs twenty times a day.

Next morning Mr. Jeffs finished installing the sink and new vanity and was wrestling with the toilet. When I went to the door to offer him coffee, he was frowning. "There's no water coming into the tank, Missus."

Ginna clattered downstairs. "Holly, I can't flush the toilet upstairs. There's no water."

I stuck my head into the living room, where Ben was stripping wallpaper. "I think the well is dry."

He came back from outside looking gloomy. "Not dry exactly, but the level is below the intake pipe."

"Now what'll we do?"

"Phone Cal and see if he has any answers."

As I reached for it, the phone rang. "Hi, Holly! We've got two weeks off and we're coming to help with the reno!" It was Gareth, Ben's son. Ingrate that I was, I could only think that now I'd be cooking for six people, three cats and a corgi that never stopped eating.

"Why don't you wait a couple of days?" I asked. "Our well ran dry this morning."

"Too late now," he said, cheerful as ever, "we just got off the ferry. We'll be there in twenty minutes."

I told him to use the bathroom in the terminal before they left, and phoned Cal Peterson.

"Not surprised," he said. "Been no rain the last three weeks. Gotta go easy on water in the summer."

"But Ben has to water the garden!"

"With that well, you can either water the garden or flush the toilets. Take your pick."

"I'll remember that for next year, but right now I've got a problem. There'll be six of us in the house for the next week or two."

"No big deal. Joe Dumont down at Ellis Bay has a water tanker. He'll bring up a load and fill the well."

Mr. Dumont allowed as how he could fill the well by midafternoon, but recommended we ration water for awhile. I went out to the veranda and edged my way through the furniture to seek comfort in the sea view. It didn't help. All I could think of was the Ancient Mariner's "water, water everywhere and not a drop to drink." Not a drop to flush with either.

Mr. Jeffs found me brooding. "Can't do much until there's water, Missus. I'll come back in a day or so."

I didn't like the sound of 'or so.' "Could you have a look at the laundry tubs? They're about a thousand years old and I'd like some new ones."

My ploy worked. Mr. Jeffs began removing the old laundry tubs and telling me about some second-hand 'like new' tubs he might be able to get for me. By three Mr. Dumont's truck had filled the well with water and Ben had filled Mr. Dumont's pocket with cash. As I expected, Ben went in to fuss with his budget after this unexpected cash outlay. Mr. Jeffs tested the downstairs toilet and pronounced it fit to use.

I put signs on both bathroom doors. 'If it's brown, flush it down, if it's yellow, let it mellow.' I could take laundry into the laundromat in Mora Bay and while the sheets were spinning, make my regular trips to the hardware, lumber store and grocery. I began making a list for next day.

"Don't worry, Holly, we'll make out fine. Just like camping." Sue had wandered into the kitchen, Beanbag at her heels. Clyde and Jeremy followed at a safe distance, fascinated by a dog who was afraid of them. "We can go in the pool instead of having showers."

"And I can use paper plates. I'd suggest everyone drink beer instead of water but I don't want any of you falling off ladders."

"Did somebody say 'beer'?" Tom thumped in wearing swim trunks. "I'm about ready for a dip in the pool."

George followed me into the bedroom and lectured me while I changed into my shorts.

"What do you want, sweetie? I know your entire kingdom is upside down, your routine is a shambles and you're repelling invaders, but your faithful slaves still belong to you."

He expressed his opinion by throwing up a hair ball on the new bedroom carpet.

***

The renovation went on apace. Ben, Tom, Ginna, Gareth, Sue, Cal and Mr. Jeffs bombarded me with questions for which I usually didn't have answers. The cats and Beanbag wanted to be fed so often I felt like I was running a fast food restaurant. The humans kept throwing dirty laundry in the general direction of the washer. That was confusing; except for Ben's and mine, I didn't know who belonged to what.

Every morning I gathered up clothes on and around the washer and stuffed them in pillow cases to take to the laundromat. I could never remember which jeans had to be hung to dry and which were allowed to go in the dryer, and my patience was stretched to the limit by whoever persisted in leaving socks in a smelly rolled-up ball.

After two days, I quit trying to sort the clothes I'd folded at the laundromat. I stacked the piles on the kitchen counter and told everyone to come and collect their own. The third day, Mr. Jeffs, who'd been crawling around under the house inspecting pipes, looked in the laundry room and complained that he couldn't find his shirt. He came into the kitchen, saw the neatly folded item on the counter and said, "Why did you wash that?"

One more question I didn't have an answer for.

George eased up on disciplining Clyde and Jeremy and went back to hunting. One morning he brought in a small green frog and released it under the dining room table, which was temporarily residing in the Ben's den. He walked off, black tail high and waving, to do whatever private things emperors do when they celebrate a triumph.

I had no wish to step on a frog, dead or alive, so I crawled under the table on my hands and knees and tried to capture it. The frog sat still until I was within two feet of it, then leapt six feet sideways. I recoiled, banging my head on the table. With much swearing, I managed to herd the creature across the hall, through the kitchen and out the open

French doors. It disappeared into the grass in the back yard, and George, who had been watching my inept attempts to capture prey, began stalking it.

"Your Royal Highness, stop! There is lunch to be made and drywall dust to be vacuumed. I don't have time to chase your little playmates out of the house."

Fortunately for me — and the frog — George spied Ben on a ladder, nailing new cedar siding over the old. The Royal Hunter went nimbly up the ladder and perched at Ben's feet, yelling at him to move so he could get a closer look at the Houseboy's handiwork. A few seconds later, Clyde and Jeremy were up there, too.

"Holly, get these cats down. I'm afraid they'll fall and hurt themselves."

The cats were all of three feet off the ground. Ben knew perfectly well they wouldn't get hurt jumping off the ladder, but his fatherly instincts had been working overtime ever since George made him Houseboy. I coaxed the cats down with tuna and life returned to its normal chaos.

Later, preparing for cocktail hour at the pool, I heard a squeal from that direction. When I went out, everyone, including the cats and Beanbag, was peering into the pool. Circling in it was a small green frog, looking worried.

"I suppose that's George's frog," I said. "Take the animals in the house and I'll get the frog out."

Three indignant cats and one reluctant dog were chivvied out of sight. The frog didn't even wait for me to grab the pool rake. He leapt out and dove into the bushes. I called the others and relaxed with my martini, hoping the frog had moved next door or across the road.

"Any progress on naming the farm?" Gareth asked.

"Cat Heaven?" Ginna said. "Holly's spoiling them rotten."

"How about Cock Crow?" Tom had changed his mind about the farm being peaceful after Mr. Mighty greeted the dawn at length three mornings in a row.

Ben looked up from his daily expense notebook. "I've got a better one. 'Destitution Dell.'"

IX - THE BLACK PLAGUE

"**Let's** go away for a week," I said. "I feel as if I'd done a year's work in the last four months. Besides, I really need a break from this place."

Ben gave me a worried look. "I suppose we could. You have been working hard."

Our relatives had gone home at the end of July, leaving the lower floor of the house looking brand new, but it had taken days to arrange the furniture, put up curtains and organize the kitchen, not to mention the time I spent gloating over my new stove and fridge. It had taken George almost as long to stop searching the house for invaders and exult over having his kingdom and staff to himself again.

"What'll we do about poor little George?" the Houseboy asked. "He'll be lonely with both of us gone. Maybe you should go away by yourself so I can stay with him. Then I'll take my turn later."

"Ben, we can't put our lives on hold for George. I suspect that having his own territory is as important to him as we are. He'll just have to cope with someone else caring for him."

We phoned Cal Peterson. He said he'd be happy to look after George, the garden and the chickens for a few days. "It'll be pay back time in September," he said, "when I do the rounds of the fall fairs."

After three glorious days in Victoria, visiting friends, I quit grumbling about the way livestock and gardens tie one down. Lazing at Long Beach on the west coast of Vancouver Island was even more relaxing and, when Ben suggested we come back two days early, I was disappointed but not unhappy. I'd missed George much more than I thought I would.

We arrived after midnight and went straight to bed, accompanied by George, who alternately ignored and scolded us for leaving him all alone. When he decided we'd had enough punishment, he curled himself around the top of my head and purred. The house, which had been locked up most of the time, was so hot we yanked the blankets off the bed and slept naked.

So much for the joys of home and hearth. I woke covered with itchy flea bites and deduced, as I tried unsuccessfully to scratch all of them at once, that the cats and Beanbag had brought fleas into the house on their fur. While we were gone, eggs had hatched, releasing hundreds of fleas with nothing to nibble on but George. Starved of food for a week, the fleas had been desperate enough to do Superman leaps onto the bed to get at me. Ben had only a few bites and I was unreasonably annoyed to learn they didn't bother him at all.

"I hate fleas even more than mosquitoes," I said to Ben, as I went on scratching. "You know my skin reacts violently to insect bites. Aside from wearing a wet suit, I don't know what to do about it. At least I can wear knee-high rubber boots to mow the lawn."

"The neighbours will think that's pretty funny."

"I don't care what they think. And I'm calling Pied Piper right this minute."

"Before you make coffee?" Ben asked plaintively. Then, more seriously, "Are you sure we need Pied Piper? I didn't budget for flea extermination."

"You wouldn't be worrying about the budget if you had to experience the agony of itchy bites all over your body or the horror of seeing little black terrorists leaping at you from the carpet."

"Why do they bite you and not me?"

"My blood smells so good that they look on me as a delicious dessert after they've chewed on George. Mother fleas tell their babies, 'Go get her; she's yummy!'"

"Can't you put something on your skin to stop them?"

"I've tried all the remedies and none of them work."

"There must be something. Go surf the Web, see what you can find out. I really don't want Pied Piper if we can find a cheaper way of dealing with the problem."

The Internet provided some interesting but useless information. I didn't need to know that a flea can jump a hundred and fifty times its body length, which is like a human jumping the length of three football fields, and do it thirty thousand times without stopping for breath. And I really didn't want to know that they can also consume up to fifteen times their body weight in blood every day.

In the vet's office, I read pamphlets on fleas and flea sprays and didn't know whether to laugh or cry. They all said, 'treat the pet's bedding as thoroughly as the floor.'

"Those tracts must be written by people who own dogs or horses," I said to Jerry. "Cats not only sleep 18 hours a day, they sleep everywhere." The flea treatment would have to be applied to the floor, all the furniture and shelving, the computer, Ben's newspapers and me.

Jerry suggested I spray or powder George. I was doubtful about George's reaction but I said I'd try.

George hated the chemical smells and the indignity of being treated. Rubbing flea powder on him required at least eight hands. Spraying didn't work because he'd immediately sit down and lick the wretched stuff off. Then be sick to his stomach on the living room carpet.

I followed the rules in the pamphlets and vacuumed everything in sight. I laundered everything that could be laundered. I used flea spray on the furniture and carpets but there was no way to prevent fleas coming into the house on cat fur or human shoes. The fleas bit George and me – and leapt, satiated, to the floor – but eventually they died. After laying their eggs, of course. I wanted to spray the whole farm, but logic dictated that if I wanted to get rid of the flea problem completely I'd have to spray the entire world, and Ben would say he hadn't budgeted for it.

Using a flea comb helped a little because George's fur was short and he adored attention, but he wouldn't allow me to use the comb on his tummy or inside his legs.

The fleas compounded the problem by refusing to cooperate. When I used the comb, I tried to catch and squeeze them to death between thumb and forefinger, but they moved too fast and seemed encased in steel. I tried slicing them in two with my thumbnail against the flea comb. This only worked when they didn't see me coming. Finally I discovered that a few cat hairs in the comb got the fleas so tangled up they couldn't move freely. It was a great pleasure dunking the comb into a pan of water and watching the brutes drown.

The basic problem, though, was persuading the King to sit still for flea-combing. Worse, fleas leapt off the comb onto me instead of back onto him. While I was frantically trying to find the fleas and get them off, George would wander away and I'd have to start all over again.

Fear of being bitten was worse, in some ways, than the bites. George and I were frightened every time we saw a small dark speck. The King, thinking he'd seen a flea in the carpet, would look for it while trying to keep all four feet off the floor at once. Unable to do this, he'd traverse the room via the furniture, peering nervously at the carpet as he leapt from item to item. When he ran out of furniture, his quick flight across the rug looked like some new high-stepping dance. This did nothing for his usual air of regal hauteur but for once in his life he was more concerned about his skin than his dignity. I knew exactly how he felt.

Twitching is contagious and soon I was leaping sideways and tempted to walk on top of the furniture myself. Cigarette smoke, according to legend, will deter insects but being a walking smudge pot didn't help at all. My only relief was to retire to a bathtub full of hot water where I could hide in safety for a while and wonder if a doctor would agree to replace my blood with some that was flea-repellent. If he could get funding for research, I was more than willing to offer myself as a guinea pig.

Ben, meanwhile, was having his own problems; while we'd been away, the deer had been munching peas and beans and corn in the garden.

"I've decided not to put up a roadside stand until the root vegetables are ready," he said. "The deer haven't left enough of the other stuff to make it worthwhile." He shook his head. "They do far more damage than I expected. I'd hoped to maybe break even this year but it isn't going to happen."

"I can freeze or can what we do get," I said, "and give some to Cal."

"It just doesn't work, having someone else look after the place," he said. "A farm needs someone around all the time and Cal has his own work to do. But it will be different when I get the puppy trained. I'll pick him up as soon as Pied Piper gets rid of the black plague." Ben had called the exterminators himself, his sympathy for George and me having overcome his budget concerns.

"You'd better get him and George each a flea collar."

"Maybe I should buy one for you." He was grinning.

"Don't be ridiculous. You can't have put that in the budget."

He stopped grinning and checked his list. "I'm going to buy bird feeders, too."

"I thought you were against feeding animals that don't pay their way."

"There won't be much for them to eat during the winter," Ben said. "I wouldn't want them to starve when a little grain will keep them going."

"Next thing you'll be feeding the deer."

"Never!" He peered at me over his glasses. "Birds aren't totally useless, you know. They eat fleas."

***

Ben had a swim in the pool the day after we came home but, when he tried to close the pool cover, it wouldn't budge. He examined the small motor that operated the heavy polyethylene cover and shook his head. "I don't know what's wrong with it. Might be a short. Might be anything."

"Maybe Cal knows how to fix it."

"I'll get him to look at it tomorrow." Ben shrugged. "Don't suppose it'll hurt to leave the cover open overnight. Not that I have any choice."

In the morning I glanced at the pool and it shimmered in the sunshine as usual, inviting now that I was actually going in it to avoid the fleas. Anticipating my afternoon dose of flea-free water, I headed upstairs to tidy the bedrooms and bath. The second floor looked shabbier than ever in contrast with the fresh paint and new flooring downstairs. Renovating up here would keep Ben busy all winter. Perhaps for the two winters we'd be here, depending on how he had budgeted the costs. With luck, we'd recoup the costs when we sold.

As I was making up the bed in the largest bedroom, I noticed a mouse on the window sill between the glass and the outside screen. The windows upstairs were old-fashioned, hinged at the bottom and opening into the room from the top. I didn't know how the little gray beast had found his way in, but I wanted him out. I shut the window, confining him, and considered the problem.

I saw no way of letting the mouse escape into the outside world except by taking the screen off from the outside, which meant climbing a ladder. Could mice cling to cedar siding? The thought that it might use me as a pathway down the ladder to freedom was daunting. Besides, there was a Royal Hunter in residence. I woke George from his morning nap and carried him upstairs.

"Do your duty, George." I opened the window, hoisted him over the top, dropped him on the sill and shut the window again. I headed for the door, not wanting to witness the carnage, but couldn't resist looking around to see if anything was happening.

George sat at one end of the sill, placidly gazing at the mouse. The mouse sat at the other end, staring at George. I blinked, sure I was hallucinating, but they hadn't moved. Then they edged to the centre, sniffed one another, and swapped corners.

Thinking it might fluster George to have me watch his foul deed, I went to the kitchen. A rejuvenating cup of coffee brought me back to sanity. George had never been embarrassed by anything except falling off the furniture when someone was watching. Even then, he did such a good job of pretending he really meant to fall that no one could have guessed he was mortified.

When I went back upstairs fifteen minutes later they'd done nothing but switch corners again.

"George," I said, "you have a reputation as the mightiest hunter in the land. You have despatched more mice than I care to remember. Why won't you do this one in?"

He looked at me and yawned.

Been there, done that.

I gave up and took George from the window enclosure. He strolled downstairs, obviously intending to finish his nap. There was only one thing to do. I yelled for the Houseboy.

He came upstairs with a small paper bag.

"Are you going to kill it?"

"Of course not. Poor little thing deserves a chance." He shooed the mouse into the bag, went downstairs and let it loose in the orchard. It fled into the blackberry vines beside Cal's fence without a backward glance.

"If that mouse had owned a bell, George would have been wearing it," I said.

"He probably thought it was your mouse. He's too much of a gentleman to steal someone else's prey."

***

Pied Piper arrived one morning and sprayed the house. George and I played on the beach most of the day, waiting for the air to clear. It was wonderful to walk back into the house knowing we wouldn't be attacked by savage little black specks. However, Ben wasn't quite so happy. Between paying Pied Piper and having bought a dog house, dog dishes and a leash, his budget for the month was a mess.

"Don't forget the egg money," I teased. "That brings in at least ten to fifteen dollars a week."

Ben put down his pen, scowling. "You know I don't regard the egg money as income. It goes to offset the feed expense, that's all. When we average out the net cost of the chickens over a couple of years, I'm sure we'll be getting top grade eggs and meat for half what we'd spend in a supermarket."

It occurred to me that Ben wasn't including the cost of our labour in his calculations, but I didn't want to raise that point and spoil his fun.

On Wednesday, Ben brought home the Samoyed pup, an adorable two-month old bundle of soft, thick, white fur, bright eyes and alert ears, eager to make friends with everyone. He bounded over to George, tail wagging, and got a sharp smack across the nose for his trouble.

The pup scuttled back to Ben, whimpering, and George stalked from the room. He was annoyed at having his territory invaded again, but I knew he'd have the dog under his paw in no time.

"Have you thought of a name for the pup?" I asked.

"It was a lot easier than naming the farm." Ben picked up the puppy and soothed him. "He's called Nicky, after the dog I had when I was a kid. Let's go walk around the farm, Nicky, and you can learn what you have to guard."

Off they went, Nicky frisking around Ben's feet, and I put on my blackberry-picking armour. Heavy denim jeans, long-sleeved jacket, rubber boots, and a scarf over my hair so the thorns wouldn't snag it. In our five months on the farm, we'd learned that even black thumbs couldn't kill a blackberry vine. Axes weren't much good either. I didn't really mind because the ripe, juicy blackberries were delicious. But the vines didn't give up their berries without a fight; they stabbed and strangled on contact.

That evening, after freezing two dozen containers of blackberries, I said, "Are you sure Nicky will be all right out in his dog house? He's just a baby."

"Dogs are supposed to sleep outside."

That didn't last long. Nicky howled non-stop and neither of us could stand it. Ben brought him in and tried to settle him on the mat at the back door, but the pup was having none of that, nor would he stay in the blanket-padded box Ben put beside our bed. He finally stopped whimpering when Ben let him up on the bed beside us.

George arched his back and growled. Nicky snuggled into the safety of Ben's arms. George walked over, sniffed the cowering pup, and returned to my pillow.

"You may have to get used to it, George," Ben said. "My dog book says Samoyeds slept in the reindeer herders' tents and helped keep them warm. Nicky's racial memories tell him that big happy families all sleep in the same bed."

"Fleas think so, too." I gave George a soothing stroke. "Good thing our bed is king-sized."

X - LIFE'S LITTLE LESSONS

One of the irritating things about small islands is that time seems to run slower than in the city, particularly for tradesmen. Since Cal couldn't fix the pool cover motor, we called in an expert from Victoria, who promised to come 'right away.' He arrived ten days later. I groused to Ben that 'instantly' probably meant five days.

In the meantime, Ben swam every afternoon, competing with leaves, dead flies and, to my horror, the odd cruising snake. At first he was willing to spend the necessary half hour skimming the pool but the novelty soon wore off and he conceded victory to the wildlife, dead or alive.

When the pool man came we gave him lunch and fresh coffee before taking him out to look at the pool. He looked, fixed the motor, and gave us a bill for $700.

Ben enjoyed his dip in a clean pool that afternoon but I didn't take my usual pleasure in the pool-side sunshine and fresh martini. The pool and its problems were annoying me. "Why don't we fill this thing with soil and plant a flower garden?"

Ben stared at me. "You've got to be joking. We have this beautiful, luxurious pool and you want to make a garden out of it?"

"Well, yes, I ...."

"And who is this 'we', white woman? It would be me planting the garden because plants shrivel up and die the minute you look at them."

I ignored the insult and went on. "We'll have to shut it down for winter soon and the weather won't be warm enough for you to go swimming again until May. Besides, the thing is way more expensive to keep up than I thought it would be. I can understand paying for feed, fertilizer and fences but putting it into this pool is like pouring it down a drain."

"Nicky loves it as much as I do," Ben said.

"We can't cough up $700 every five minutes just so Nicky can have a swimming pool." The pup clambered out of the pool and shook himself all over George, who stalked away, swearing.

"You'd better dry him off before he runs into the house," I said. The pup had poked his nose at the cat flap, learned that it moved, and had been scooting in and out that way ever since. George was using it more, too, though he still preferred his bedroom window entrance.

Agitated clucking and squawking from the direction of the henhouse brought us to our feet. When we reached it, Mr. Mighty was strutting back and forth, preventing a clutch of nervous but curious hens from going inside.

Ben peered in and said, "A rat! Get George."

When I came back with George, Ben said, "I think it's a young one. It doesn't seem frightened of me."

"I hope it's afraid of George." I put the King down and he sauntered in.

Instead of pouncing, George sat in front of the rat and stared at it. The rat stared at George. They got up, touched noses and each backed away a foot. After a moment George turned around and sauntered out again.

"Where's your hunting instinct?" I demanded.

He looked up at me as if to say, "Where's yours?" and wandered off to the orchard.

Ben swore, got a shovel and killed the rat himself. Nicky watched and, when Ben gave him the rat's body to sniff, flipped it into the air and 'killed' it a dozen times before we could make him release it.

"That's good training for him." Ben put the shovel away. "He might turn into a better ratter than George."

"The way George brings in trophies nearly as big as he is, I thought he'd be delighted with another rat."

"If that cat had been a lion in an ancient Roman amphitheatre and walked away from a fight like that, he'd have been a rug on the emperor's floor quicker than it takes to cook asparagus."

"Where'd you get the asparagus comparison?"

"The emperor Augustus used to say it." Ben shook his head. "Maybe George is only interested in game he stalks himself. That's twice he's refused to kill something you've cornered for him."

"In other words, it's the thrill of the hunt that he likes, not the killing." I returned to the pool and my now warm martini. It was also more than possible that George simply liked to be contrary now and again to remind us who held the imperial sceptre.

***

We'd had plenty of rain in late summer but in early September the weather turned hot and dry and the garter snakes seemed to multiply overnight. One day I caught a glimpse of George on the driveway, carrying one toward the house. I raced around closing all the doors and windows, including his cat door, so he couldn't bring it inside, then went to the laundry room window to watch his progress, which was much slower than usual.

George gripped the middle of the snake's body in his mouth so that the head and tail both dragged on the ground. At almost every step, he stumbled over one or the other, which jerked his head down so that he nearly lost his grip. The snake reacted by waving its head and tail back and forth and George would manage another couple of steps unimpeded.

By the time he disappeared around the side of the house I was laughing so hard I could barely find breath to ask Ben to separate George from his latest prey.

"I wish you were less squeamish," the Houseboy said. "He's made it quite clear that he's your cat, so you should have the honour of releasing his trophies."

"All right, but I'll have to go to Mora Bay and buy gardening gloves. I couldn't touch a live snake with my bare hands. Or a dead one, either."

Ben muttered a profanity and went off to deal with the snake.

I went off to the veranda to dispose of the cherry tomato plants. The pitiful harvest had proved to Ben once and for all that I had black thumbs. For an investment of twenty dollars and hours of my labour, Ben had collected ten tiny tomatoes. Even the jade plant Sue had given me was slowly withering. I seemed to have a black thumb when it came to writing, too. The last story had been rejected as quickly as the first. I had no intention of giving up, though; in my current story I'd killed off my lawyer ex-boss, a most satisfactory revenge for all the trouble he'd caused me.

Much of Ben's two acres of garden had been mauled by the deer and we still had to chase them out almost every day. When I went after them, they'd jump smartly over to the next row and keep on eating. Nicky, still a roly-poly baby, barked bravely at them from behind me, but they merely lowered their heads and snorted at him. I'd grown hoarse from shouting and frustrated to the point where I wanted to buy a gun so we could have a freezer full of deer meat.

The tins of urine placed around the perimeter and tufts of hair tied to barbed wire, as suggested by Cal, hadn't done a darn thing. Except embarrass Ben when he showed off what was left of his neat rows of vegetables to giggling guests.

When Ben returned from depositing the wriggling snake into the neighbour's field, I said, "I think you'll have to give in and build a higher fence around the garden."

"Nicky will take care of the deer once he's a little bigger."

"Uh huh. That dog is a wimp."

Ben picked up the puppy and cuddled him. "Don't bad-mouth my guard dog. He'll be fine once I've trained him."

The training thus far had consisted of Ben saying firmly to the dog, "Heel!" and Nicky wagging his tail and bouncing around Ben's feet. Then Ben would say in a conciliatory tone, "Heel, Nicky, okay?"

George was doing a much better job than Ben. In the evenings we restricted Nicky to the kitchen and laundry room by blocking the cat door and the other two doors with sheets of plywood. Ben put newspaper on the floor to take care of his still frequent 'accidents' while assuring me that as soon as the pup was older, he'd learn to tell us when he wanted to go out. George didn't mind this arrangement; he could easily get to his litter box in the laundry room by leaping over the plywood.

One night we'd been watching a thriller on television when we heard Nicky yelping in the pen. We dashed down the hall and peered in. George was herding the pup toward the litter box with well-aimed smacks on the bum. As soon as the pup was in the litter box, George sat by while Nicky obediently pooped in the sand. Then the pup watched with great interest while George covered it up. This had happened several times since.

I threw the dead tomato plant skeletons in the compost box and said to Ben, "You and George are doing such a good job of training Nicky that I'll leave you to it. And now there's less to do around here I've got time to try my hand at something else artistic. A night class on drawing starts in Mora Bay at the end of this month."

Ben said, "I hope you draw better than you raise tomatoes."

***

The grasshoppers seemed to multiply in the hot weather, too, and George sometimes ate so many he didn't want his supper. One afternoon he trotted into the kitchen with the usual spindly legs sticking out of his mouth.

"George, I don't think that's a grasshopper. The legs are black, not green."

He ignored me and crunched the insect. At once he spat it out and backed away, hissing. I picked it up in a paper towel, inspected it and put it in the garbage. "That was a cricket. Didn't it taste good?"

No answer. George, eyes crossed, was busy sticking his tongue out of his mouth as though trying to spit the taste off it. I followed him to the bathroom where he drank, then shook his head, spraying drops everywhere. Struggling between laughter and empathy, I offered him a cat candy. He glared at me. A couple of hours later he was still trying to get rid of his tongue.

Ben said, "I bet he's learned the difference between crickets and grasshoppers." George headed for his bathroom water dish again and Ben grinned. "We'll have to hire a taster for His Majesty. If the budget can stand it."

George was fine by the following day, when Cal came over for coffee. "I'm going to Vancouver Island tomorrow," he said. "Got some entries for the fall fair at Saanichton."

I assumed he was taking some of his Angora goats. I'd seen them over the fence a few times and they were like walking balls of wool with four little feet sticking out the bottom and two horns sticking out the top. Occasionally a yellow eye glared at me from behind a dishevelled fringe.

"Want us to look after your place?" Ben asked.

"If you wouldn't mind. I'll only be gone three days."

We followed Cal to his place to learn what needed to be done. Cal had never invited us to his house, apparently preferring the coffee and cookies at ours, and I was curious to see how he lived.

His house was ancient, the logs weathered to silver and topped by the mossy shake roof I'd seen over the blackberry barrier. Ben and Cal both had to duck to enter the front door. Inside was a large room, with a couple of doors at the far end leading to bedroom and bathroom.

"My folks built this place when they settled here," he said. "Must be eighty-five years old. Kinda dark because the windows are so small, but it suits me."

When my eyes adjusted to the dimness, I saw a large loom in the centre of the room along with a spinning wheel and untidy piles of wool. On the wall were hangings of woven wool, in beautiful designs and clear, pure colours. "Who did those?"

Cal looked a little embarrassed. "I do them. In my spare time. That's what I'm taking to the fair."

"They're gorgeous," I said. "I thought you were taking some of the goats."

"I raise the goats for wool, not to show."

"Must take a lot of work to get the wool to where you can use it," Ben said. "How often do you shear them?"

"Twice a year. Then I wash the wool and card it and spin it and dye it. Kinda fun once you figure out how."

I was liking Cal better all the time. His macho Mister Fix-It exterior was only a protective mask for his artistic interior. Now I knew why he and Sylvia lived apart. He didn't want to leave his goats or his weaving and I couldn't imagine any woman wanting to live in the untidy squalor of his old log house.

By the time we'd been introduced to the goats and Daisy, the multi-coloured cat, and given our instructions, I realized I'd seen his work at an artisan's gallery in Mora Bay. I was even more impressed. Next day Cal caught the early ferry and Ben and I took over as goat-keepers.

The job wasn't as hard as I'd feared. The Angoras cropped grass and blackberry vines and all we had to do was feed them in stalls once a day and give them drinking water. We took Nicky with us and the sight of one tiny ball of white fluff trying to herd a dozen big ones had us laughing so hard our chores took twice as long.

"I told you he'd be okay," Ben said. "Herding goats can't be much different than herding reindeer, which is what his ancestors did."

Nicky liked his job so much we had a hard time getting him home each day, though the goats chased him as much as he did them. The Angoras seemed to like our company, too, and followed us to the gate that separated their range from the house yard every time we left.

"Do you suppose they'd follow us home?" Ben asked.

"Don't even say it! How would we ever get them back in their pen? Nicky's not big enough yet to be much help. You're not thinking of raising goats, too, are you?"

He shook his head. "I've got enough to do raising cats and chickens and a garden for the deer."

"I still think you should build a higher fence."

"If it turns out Nicky can't control the deer, I guess I'll have to." Ben patted my arm. "I knew when we moved here that this first year might end up being a learning experiment. I'm not expecting to make any money now, just learn what we have to do to make the garden a success. Next year will prove whether or not I can do it."

When Cal returned, he came over to thank us with a piece of material he'd woven. "Be about the right amount for a skirt," he said. He also admitted shyly that he'd won first prize at the fair for one of his wall hangings.

"I'd like to see it," I said.

"Can't. I sold it." He added proudly, "Got $1,500 for it, too."

Ben's eyes widened. "Maybe there's something to this Angora goat business."

I had a chilling vision of myself washing, carding, spinning and dyeing endless piles of mohair. "I have enough to do combing the tangles out of Nicky's fur. And you need to teach him to herd deer. We don't have time for goats."

Ben's eyes twinkled. "Just checking."

***

Ben called from the living room, "There's a strange cat in the front yard."

I joined him at the window. A large short-haired cat with a black face and a black and white body sat near the veranda and stared back at us. "He looks thin. I'll put out some food and water for him."

"You told me once that feeding a stray meant you'd have him forever," Ben said. "We don't need another cat."

"But I want one. The trouble is, George might not let me keep him. He tolerated Clyde and Jeremy, though."

"That's only because Clyde and Jeremy had their own slaves and didn't try to steal us away from him."

I put food and water on the veranda and the cat, whom we named Blackjack, took to sleeping under it. George called him rude names and ran him off the property a dozen times a day, but Blackjack seemed to sense when George was sleep and always came sneaking back.

One day Blackjack strolled into the house and ate out of George's dish. The King suddenly emerged from the linen closet, saw the other cat and went for him. Blackjack got out barely in time and disappeared for the rest of the day.

"Why is George so determined to chase Blackjack away?" Ben asked. "He can still be King."

"I guess he's afraid if he shares his empire and slaves he'll end up losing everything."

Blackjack and I persisted, but George refused to soften his attitude. As far as he was concerned, it was a one-cat kingdom; he had troubles enough controlling his slaves and Nicky.

After the third confrontation at the food dish in the kitchen, Ben said, "I don't think this is going to work. George is never going to give in."

"He'll have to, sometime."

Next time we locked George in the bathroom before we invited Blackjack inside to eat. Blackjack was cautious but after eating, he checked out the kitchen and living room and decided it was safe. He sprawled on the rug, purring, his eyes half shut in contentment.

Ben went to the bathroom and let George out.

Fortunately, we'd left the front door open far enough for Blackjack to escape. He disappeared into the blackberries, George right behind him.

"It's no good," Ben said. "We'll have to find another home for Blackjack."

"I hate to give up. He's such an easy-going little guy. I'm worried about what will happen to him."

We phoned around and for once, luck was with us. The Frasers at Ellis Bay, who had sold us the chickens and Nicky, wanted to adopt a cat. Our experience with George had made us so cunning there was no trouble putting Blackjack into the cat carrier. He meowed softly a few times on the trip down to Ellis Bay, but remained calm in spite of the bumpy road.

"He's so civilized I'm beginning to think we should have taken George instead," I said.

Ben looked startled. "You don't mean that."

"Of course I don't mean it. I'm just griping about everybody but us having laid-back cats."

"But George has more personality than a dozen other cats put together."

"I remember when you thought cats had no personality."

Ben shook his head. "I had no idea they were such fascinating animals."

I sighed. It was a little crushing to realize every story I'd ever told him about cats had gone in one ear and out the other, but it was exactly the same thing that happened with my commands to George.

We left Blackjack with his head stuck in a food bowl, his adoptive parents gazing fondly at him.

The moment we entered the house, George tore up the stairs and back down again. He raced back and forth in the hall and chased imaginary prey. Once or twice he stopped and, legs braced, tail lashing, gave us a wild-eyed, puckish look. Then off he went again.

"Vacuum activity," said the Houseboy, who had by now read every book on cats he could find. "He has a safe place to live and plenty of food, so his energy builds up because he doesn't have to patrol territory and hunt the way wild cats do."

"But why 'vacuum'?"

"You know the saying 'nature abhors a vacuum.' There's a vacuum — an empty space — in George's life due to lack of exercise, so nature fills it by causing him to race around at full speed."

"That's much too scientific. I'd prefer to think he's chasing elephants."

"I'm sure he would, too. I just hope he never catches one because you'd stick me with the job of getting rid of it."

XI - FALL SURPRISES

October was balmy, the mornings fresh with dew and spider webs sparkling in the sun. By ten we were outside in the mellow warmth harvesting potatoes, carrots and beets or finishing off the cedar siding on the house. The big maples in our little forest had turned into golden splashes of sunshine against the dark evergreens. With a blue sky overhead, blue sea shimmering a quarter mile away and hens clucking contentedly to each other in the orchard while Ben pruned fruit trees, I felt almost reconciled to life on a small island farm. Almost.

Even George the Magnificent was mellow. He'd given Nicky a few swift smacks to teach the dog who was boss and, though Nicky now weighed twice as much as George, he still deferred to the King. They roamed the farm together every day, George giving the dog lessons in hunting.

"I think Nicky catches more mice than George," Ben said. His training of Nicky had not progressed beyond the 'Sit, Nicky, okay?' stage but the pup was smart and I thought he might eventually make a good watch dog.

"When are you going to teach him to chase the deer?"

"He tried to herd Cal's goats. He'll herd the deer when he's bigger."

Fortunately, Nicky was good-natured and a sharp 'No!' had so far kept him from sins like chewing my slippers and climbing on the couch but nothing I could do kept him off our bed. He continued to use the cat door, though it was a struggle because of his expanding girth. He'd poke his head out, look both ways for traffic, then suck in his belly and wriggle through.

One day I saw George coming across the lawn, stumbling over the garter snake dragging from his mouth. I blocked the cat flap and had just shut George's window entrance when I heard a heavy thud and a yip. Nicky had obviously tried to fire himself through the cat flap. When I opened the door and told him he was getting too big for it, he looked at me with hurt surprise and went off to look for comfort from Ben. We were back to being butlers again.

Other things had improved, however. "I notice George hasn't thrown up much lately," Ben said. "Are you feeding him something different?"

"No. He seems more confident now. He should be; we've had him almost seven months." Being a little superstitious, I didn't want to voice my fear that George was saving his energy to do it at Christmas, when he could impress guests and keep me even busier than the season warranted.

Ben read my mind. "We'd better not give him much turkey at Christmas or he'll be at it again, like the ancient Roman aristocracy at their banquets. They induced vomiting so they could go on eating."

"Disgusting."

"I bet George doesn't think so."

"Don't tell him that," I said. "He understands human language quite well when he wants to. The problem is that he usually doesn't want to. He doesn't hear a word when I tell him to get off my drawing assignments."

"He's probably trying to help you."

"I might as well let him; George's wet foot prints are more artistic than anything I can do with a pencil. I don't really mind. At least I know now that I can't draw worth a darn."

"Or grow tomatoes," Ben added.

George was most indignant when the weather turned cold in November and we had to shut our bedroom window. Speeding toward the house at full gallop, as usual, he slammed into the window three midnights in a row. Then swore loudly enough to wake us up – as if we hadn't already been wakened by the crash and the shuddering glass – and issued shrill orders to be let in. Ben and I pretended not to hear him, knowing that eventually he'd go round to the cat door. We also pretended not to hear the lengthy lecture we received when he landed on the bed and paced back and forth across the Houseboy, Nicky and me.

I tried to atone by letting him sleep in the bottom drawer of my dresser on Cal's mohair cloth, which George loved. That was a mistake; every time I went to the bathroom in the night, I tripped over the open drawer. I finally moved the cloth to a cardboard box in the corner.

"I hope Cal never comes in here and sees you've given his first prize weaving to George for a blanket," Ben said. "Why don't you make it into a skirt, like Cal suggested?"

"I will. I just want to strengthen it with a little cat hair first."

***

Near the end of the month, Jerry Parker, the veterinarian, phoned. "Holly, I've found a fourth for bridge. How's George the Magnificent?"

"He's fine. And I'm dying to trump somebody's ace. Who is it?"

"Frank Lansing, a high school teacher who retired here a few months ago. He brought his Maine Coon cat in the other day and we got talking."

I went to Jerry's place for bridge the following evening and met his wife, Cindy, and Frank Lansing. We enjoyed a good, competitive game and agreed to meet a week later at Frank's house, half a mile out of Mora Bay.

"I'm not much good at baking," he said, "but I'll find something to go with the coffee."

A large, shaggy Maine Coon cat with dark tabby colouring and wise yellow eyes stood beside Frank when he opened the door to me. "This is Jezebel," he said.

"She's gorgeous. Does she mind being picked up?"

"Not at all. She'll be insulted if you don't."

When I picked her up she started a rumbling purr. "This is one heavy cat. How much does she weigh?"

"Eight kilograms."

I did my mental arithmetic. "Eighteen pounds?"

Frank raised his eyebrows. "Another holdout from the metric system, are you? Good thing we don't use it for keeping score."

Jerry and Cindy arrived and we settled down to the game. After the first rubber was over I hurried to the bathroom and found, to my dismay, that the last person to use it hadn't flushed. Oh, well, I thought, Frank's a widower. Perhaps he's fallen into bad habits. I hoped he wouldn't be so lackadaisical at my house.

When the third rubber began, we were nearly tied for points and conversation ceased while we concentrated on the play of the hand. Suddenly, through the open bathroom door, I heard the sound of someone urinating.

Frank saw me blink in amazement and said, "Oh, that's Jezebel. She always uses the toilet. I meant to warn you."

I apologized to him silently. But lost the game because, instead of remembering to pull trumps, I was trying to figure out how to train George to use the toilet.

***

Early in December, Ben's brother in Moose Jaw called. David said their mother, who had just turned seventy-seven, had suffered a heart attack and was in hospital. Ben booked a flight out of Victoria and devoted the rest of the morning to giving me a great long list of things I was supposed to do around the farm while he was gone.

"Ben, I do know enough to feed and water the chickens every day! I've done it often enough."

Undeterred, he said, "Put a jacket on. I want to show you where I keep the wild bird feed." He'd put up half a dozen bird feeders in October. "I have to show you how to prime the pump in case the power goes off, too."

I crawled into the pump house and switched on the forty-watt bulb. Ben gave me instructions from the doorway. The procedure seemed easy enough except for the spiders and beetle-like bugs that kept me cringing and yelping.

"I wish Tom had taken time to enlarge this place," I said, inching my way out backwards.

"I'll get to it next spring," Ben promised. "Let's check the pool."

In October he'd drained enough water so that the level was beneath the outlet pipes in case the temperature dropped below freezing. The surface of the water was now more than two feet down from the lip of the pool.

Ben rolled back the cover. Everything seemed to be in order, but he added a little more salt chlorine. "You never know, it might get really cold while I'm away."

"Surely not in December. I know it will freeze in January, but this is too early." It would be all right with me if frost cracked the cement and pipes, forcing Ben to get rid of the pool rather than spend thousands of dollars on it, but it seemed mean to say so.

"Better safe than sorry." He turned on the switch to close the pool cover. Nothing happened. "Don't tell me that thing is on the fritz again!"

He and Cal spent most of the afternoon struggling with the motor. When they came in for coffee, Ben said, "We can't fix it. You'll have to phone that repairman again."

"Better get him here soon," Cal said to me. "It's dangerous to leave the pool open when the water's so low. If one of Dyckman's cows gets in there, we'll never get her out."

"I'll put Nicky on twenty-four hour guard duty."

Ben glared at me. "It's not funny. You keep an eye out for those cows."

Ben had been right about the weather. Three days after he left, the mercury dropped below freezing and I was happy to have Nicky cuddling next to me on the bed every night.

When Ben phoned, I said, "How's your Mom?"

"Better. Dave and I think she should go into a nursing home but she's determined to go back to her apartment."

Typical Edith. I hadn't spent much time in her company but it was obvious from the first that she was fiercely independent and outspoken. "Being in her own home is really important to her."

"I know. We're going to see about getting home help for her. How's the weather?"

"Cold."

Ben said, "Leave the light on in the pump house. That will generate enough heat to keep the pump working. And put a heater in the hen house."

"There's only five degrees of frost. That's not cold. On our farm up north, chickens survived forty below zero without any artificial heat."

"That can't possibly be right. Your memory must be faulty. You watch the hens and if they look cold, put a heater out there. Are they laying as many eggs?"

Next he'd be asking me to knit sweaters for the hens. "No, they're not. I've phoned our customers and told them eggs will be rationed until spring." When I said the pool motor hadn't been repaired because the expert was sunning in Acapulco, he swore and promised to be home within the week.

That night I woke to Nicky whining beside me. I shushed him, then heard an odd high-pitched squeaking that sounded to my sleepy ears like starlings fighting on the roof. As the squeaking continued, I woke up enough to remember that birds sleep at night. But what else could it be squeaking on the roof? I crawled out of bed and, with Nicky at my heels, went upstairs to see if I could hear anything more. When I glanced out the east bedroom window, cold, bright moonlight revealed a big dog thrashing around in the pool, the water level too low for him to scramble out. His whimpering was now frantic and getting louder.

I slung on dressing gown, mitts and rubber boots and, leaving Nicky inside, went to the rescue. Another dog paced nervously on the pool apron. I coaxed the first one to the side of the pool and, with a lot of heaving and swearing – and nearly falling in myself – hauled him out by the scruff of the neck. I wondered what they'd been chasing so blindly that the leader had fallen into the water before he realized it was there.

The wet dog shook himself all over me, then fled with its companion down across the meadow and into the bush. Shivering, I cursed them and turned to go into the house. The rustling of leaves in the blackberry vines beside the pool told me another animal was in hiding.

A smug little Siamese-tabby face emerged, followed by a sleek, elegant body and a black tail.

"George, did you lure those dogs into the pool?"

He flicked his tail and pranced toward the house. I could have sworn he was smiling.

Next day I phoned a pool repairman in Vancouver. It would cost more in travel time, but I didn't trust George and his devious, furry little mind. Now that he'd progressed to prey ten times his size, he might just try luring something even bigger into the pool. None of us, not even cows and deer, needed any more surprises.

XII - ST. FRANCIS

When Ben came home from Moose Jaw, the first thing he did was check the chickens, probably to make sure I hadn't starved them. Then he came in, noted the temperature had risen to five degrees Centigrade and refused to translate that to Fahrenheit so I could decide if I needed an extra sweater when I went outside. The pool motor repairman arrived, did his magic, and suggested we install a hydraulic system, at a cost that had both of us scowling.

"I still think we should fill the pool and plant spring flowers," I said.

"You mean I should plant flowers," Ben said. "Easy for you to say; you and your black thumb wouldn't be involved."

"I could water them. Anyway, it would be less nerve-wracking than worrying about the pool and we could sell the flowers to the supermarket in Mora Bay. Or from our own roadside kiosk. You said you were going to build one this winter anyway, for next year's vegetables."

"But think how much fun we had swimming last summer."

"You had fun swimming. All I ever did was sit beside it. Besides, hauling a wet dog out of the water on a freezing cold night was just about the last straw for me. Plus the worry about cows or deer falling in."

"The cover will prevent that." Ben loved the pool; it was only the hole it caused in his blasted budget that he didn't like. Somehow I had to convince him that the pool simply wasn't worth what it cost, especially with the ocean less than a quarter mile away.

We were still arguing about it on a bleak, freezing night in January, an icy wind stabbing in off the Strait of Georgia, when we heard a faint mewing at the back door.

Cowering inside the big wood shed beside the back step was a scruffy, long-haired gray cat with large golden eyes and a beautiful face. When we said hello, it ran awkwardly away on three legs, its right front leg held up as though something was wrong with it.

"I'll put some food out," Ben said. "The poor little thing's been hurt and she's probably starving to death."

"Feed a stray cat, you'll have it for life."

"I think we've had this conversation before. But I'm not going to turn away a starving cat on a night like this. George will never let her stay, anyway."

Half an hour later Ben came back in. "I put out a big bowl of kibbles and made a bed for her with a cardboard box and old towels. It's inside the wood shed, so she'll be out of the wind. If she stays, she's going to be my cat."

"How do you know it's a 'she'?"

"A male couldn't be that pretty."

"I hope George didn't hear you say that. Perhaps we should advertise to see if anyone's lost a cat."

"She's obviously been living wild for a long time. I think somebody dumped her." Ben looked fierce. "I'd like to catch whoever did it."

"Then we'll keep her, if George will allow it. And she can be your cat."

There was no doubt George was my cat; Ben was second choice even in emergencies and a lowly houseboy the rest of the time. I felt honoured to be butler, cook and surrogate mother to royalty but it took a lot of time. George was less demanding than he had been, but if I'd been away for a day he sat on my lap or my shoulders when I was writing and on my head when I slept, like a leech with claws. At such times I sometimes wondered what it would be like to have the luxury of sitting on the toilet all by myself.

Next day the gray cat came for more food. "She's quite handsome," the Houseboy said. "Well, she could be, if somebody brushed her and she gained some weight."

"I hope George is now secure enough in his position as head cat to let her stay." I thought she was beautiful, too, but I didn't want to get my hopes up and then suffer the disappointment of having George evict her.

Later Ben rushed into my studio. "Do you know what I just saw? George was sitting beside the gray cat and licking her wounded leg."

"Good! He's trying to help her heal."

"I didn't know animals did things like that." Ben paced to the other window, looking both amazed and pleased. "Then he's not just tolerating her because she's female. That settles it. We're going to adopt her."

"Do you think she'll earn her keep?" I asked, deadpan.

He looked at me as though I'd spoken in Sanskrit. "What do you mean, earn her keep? Who cares about that?"

Ben's conversion didn't surprise me but I wondered about George's newfound tolerance. He'd never give up his position as king, though his score wasn't perfect since Mr. Mighty still put him on the run. Had he really mellowed enough to share his kingdom or did his furry little head harbor some devious plan for the gray cat?

Nicky, though he now weighed forty pounds and looked bigger because of his thick fur, had learned to respect cats. He watched the gray cat with a bright-eyed curiosity but kept a safe distance from her.

In daylight she proved to be even prettier than we'd thought. Dark gray with white feet, chest and belly, she had a white blaze on her nose and a fluffy tail. Her fur was shorter than a Persian's, but longer than George's tabby coat, and hopelessly tangled with burrs and bits of dried leaves. Her yellow, slanted eyes gazed at us with both terror and longing. She looked like pictures I'd seen of Norwegian Forest cats, big, stocky, sedate felines by reputation, and I thought she might be a good antidote to George's vociferous, quicksilver nature.

Ben assumed responsibility for looking after the new cat and named her 'Henrietta' though half the time he called her 'Miss Mew' because she had such a gentle little voice.

"The ritual of naming is a secret mother cats transmit to kittens along with milk," I said. "As soon as you've named them, they know they've got you."

"I wish she'd come inside," the Houseboy said. "She must be so cold sleeping out there. I want to get a look at that wounded leg of hers, too."

However, it took Henrietta some time to decide she wanted to become Princess. She progressed from bolting her food and bolting from us, to savouring her food but keeping a safe distance. Eventually, Ben was allowed to pet her. One warm day in late February we left the back door open and she walked in, investigated, and condescended to stay for a couple of hours.

Ben was overjoyed. He rushed off to Mora Bay in Bouncing Blue Betsy and came back loaded down with catnip, cat toys, a double decker cat bunk and soft cat-sized blankets. I refrained, with difficulty, from asking if he'd budgeted for being a new father.

Outdoors, George accepted Henrietta's presence and even played with her. But if we paid too much attention to her, he'd have a fit of jealousy and I was afraid he'd chase her away permanently. I needn't have worried. Henrietta had discovered heaven: a warm house, a source of food and two willing slaves.

The next time Henrietta came in, she sat and studied Ben in his armchair for a few minutes, then leapt up and sat in his lap. He was thrilled.

"Aren't you a gorgeous girl?" he crooned. "You're my beautiful lady, aren't you?" He went on to tell her what a clever cat she was for cuddling up to him to show her gratitude for food and shelter.

"Gratitude?" I queried, astonished that living with George for almost a year hadn't taught him the true nature of the feline race.

"Henrietta is different," he said.

I held my tongue.

Next day Henrietta walked past Ben, climbed on my lap, kneaded my thighs, curled into a ball and went to sleep. I was happy; the kneading meant she was content.

"What's with her?" Ben demanded. "You've hardly paid her any attention. I'm the one who feeds her and makes her warm beds and talks to her."

"She knows I'm a Cat Person."

He said grumpily, "I suppose I'm going to be Houseboy around here for the rest of my life."

"I thought you were content with your lot."

"I am. But those two could at least show a little gratitude. Nicky does, you know. He wags his tail and licks my hand and follows me everywhere."

"Dogs need a leader to look up to. Cats don't."

Ben glared at George, who was glaring at my lapful of Henrietta. "He doesn't even greet me when I come home."

"Did Roman emperors greet their slaves when they came home from the chariot races? Or show gratitude?"

"I don't have time to sit around debating trifles," Ben said, and retreated to his den.

***

By mid-March, Henrietta had established herself as second in command and we decided it was time to put her in a cat carrier and whisk her off to the animal clinic. She still had a festering sore on her right front leg, matted fur on her belly and a broken fang. She also needed shots.

George hated the cat carrier but, though he struggled and complained so loudly I was sure that people as far away as Mora Bay thought someone was being tortured, he was fairly easy to handle – provided we grabbed him before he knew the carrier was waiting for him. Otherwise, we had to pry him out from underneath the couch or coax him from behind the old upright piano.

"We'd better sneak the carrier in the same way as we do for George," I said. "Put it on the kitchen table where Henrietta won't see it and don't let the handle rattle."

"What's the problem?" Ben asked. "There's two of us and only one of her and we're a lot bigger."

When the carrier was in place, Ben said, "Now, pick up Miss Mew and give her a little cuddle. You'll have her in the cage before she knows what's happening."

A great theory, but it bore no resemblance to reality. Within two feet of the open cage, Henrietta turned into a windmill. Head, teeth and four legs whirled in different directions, propelled by a body which had suddenly acquired superior strength. She kicked me and disappeared.

We'd locked every exit, so we knew she couldn't get out of the house, but where was she? We searched everywhere, even in places she couldn't possibly be. Or so we thought. Finally I shone a flashlight between the head of our bed frame and the wall. I couldn't imagine Henrietta squeezing herself into a space two inches wide, but there simply wasn't anywhere else to look.

Two large, slanted yellow eyes stared back at me.

Now we had a new reason for panic. Never mind how she'd got in there; how was she going to get out?

A closer look reminded me that the bottom of the headboard was six inches off the floor and the actual width between bed and wall, at floor level, was five inches. A tight squeeze, but manageable for a cat. Not for us, though. I got an arm into the tunnel but Henrietta simply backed out of reach. Ben tried from the other side but the king-size bed was too wide. Henrietta sat in the middle, untouchable. We'd just have to wait until she came out on her own.

She did, almost at once. Cats aren't stupid. A hiding place is no longer a hiding place if humans know about it.

I worried that she'd never speak to us again, but she seemed inclined to forgive and forget. Her forgiveness, I suspected, hinged on us forgetting about putting her in a small dark box.

We cancelled our appointment with the clinic and started plotting. How were we going to get this stubborn feline into a carrier? We consulted Jerry, who gave us some tranquillizers.

All the tranquillizer did was make poor Henrietta unsteady on her feet and inclined to fall down every three steps. She didn't even get drowsy. When picked up and lowered toward the cat cage, she turned into a windmill again.

"Try putting some canned tuna in the carrier," the Houseboy suggested. "She won't be able to resist that."

"Forget it," I said. "Not even tuna will make her go inside that box unless she's starving and that would take three or four days. How would you feel, refusing to feed her for such a long time?"

The guilt on his face was sufficient answer. "Where are those cat tranquillizers?"

"Why? They don't work on her."

"I'm going to take one myself."

Slaves quickly learn patience and cunning and we were no exception. We waited until Henrietta, who slept soundly, was snoozing on the couch. Then we tiptoed in with the cat carrier and very carefully lowered it to the floor in front of the couch. Holding my breath and trying to pretend I wasn't the least bit nervous, I picked her up and popped her into the cage. The Houseboy tucked her tail inside and slammed the lid down as she woke up.

"Whew! Let's hope she never needs to go to the hospital again," I said. "I don't think I could pull that off a second time."

"Oh, she'll learn it's for her own good," Ben said. "We won't have this trouble again."

"I can't believe you said that." I was grateful that Ben had fallen in love with cats, but someday he'd have to get over being naive and unduly optimistic when it came to what they would or would not do.

He peered through the tiny screened window at her and crooned, "What a sweet little lady! There's my gorgeous girl. You'll be all fixed up soon."

An hour after we left Henrietta at the clinic, Jerry phoned.

"I've done everything you asked me to do. I assume you want him neutered as well?"

"Him?"

Jerry chuckled. "Yes. It's Henry, not Henrietta."

I went outside to tell Ben, who was staring at the fence around the garden as though he could force it to grow another four feet by will power alone.

"It's a good thing you picked 'Henrietta' as a name; all we have to do is shorten it. Jerry says Henrietta is a boy."

"But I wanted a girl!"

"Guess we'll have to try again, huh?"

***

A few days later, Ben went off on a mysterious errand to Ellis Bay and returned with the tarp tied down over Blue Betsy's box. Cheeping and squawking came from underneath.

"More hens? I thought we had enough."

"These are different," Ben said, untying the ropes.

A flock of little yellow hens, with tufts of feathers on their heads but no tails at all, fluttered out, flew into the orchard and settled in the top branches of a pear tree like frowzy golden pigeons. Mr. Mighty, ever vigilant, bustled over to the tree and ordered them to come down for inspection.

"What are they? They look too small to be much good for anything."

"They're Araucanas and they come from South America."

"Do they lay eggs?"

"Little pale green ones, Mrs. Fraser says."

"People aren't going to buy little green eggs, Ben."

"We can eat them." Ben gave me a sideways glance. "I think they're kind of cute, with those little tufts on their heads."

"Wonderful. Are the eggs green inside too?"

"Of course not. Anyway, who cares?"

Ben was beginning to bear a distinct resemblance to St. Francis of Assisi.

XIII - THE ROYAL LAVATORY

We brought Henry home from the clinic, neutered, shot full of anti-rabies, anti-distemper and anti-feline leukemia serums, his right front leg bandaged from ankle to chest and the white fur on his belly half-shaved. He was so eager to get away from the clinic he climbed into the carrier all by himself.

Jerry apologized for the sloppy shaving job. Henry had come out of the anaesthetic before he could finish getting rid of the tangled, knotted fur on the cat's belly.

"You can probably snip away the rest of it yourself. Be sure to keep him inside so his bandage won't get wet. He uses a litter box, doesn't he?"

"I don't know," I said. "If not, I'll teach him."

"Good. Can you play bridge Wednesday night, my place?"

"Nothing could keep me away."

On the way home, I said to Ben, "It's not hard to teach a cat to use a litter box. I think it's almost instinctive for them to use one, anyway. George teaching Nicky to use the litter box is proof of how fastidious cats are. But the box has to be kept clean."

He looked surprised. "Are cats that fussy?"

"You don't understand George's language well enough yet to know when he's yelling for someone to clean it."

"We should get a bigger box. Eighteen kilos of dog trying to balance in a cat-sized litter box looks pretty silly."

"I wish Peri and Jezebel were here to teach both of them how to use the toilet. I've told you about Peri, haven't I?"

"Many times."

"I don't think I told you this story."

Peri was a small dark tabby with big ears and rust highlights in her fur. 'Peri' is the Persian word for fairy and I'd named her that because I thought she was dainty, delicate and subtle. It turned out that Peri had as much subtlety as a bull moose.

One evening I came home from work to find she'd defecated on the tile floor beside her litter box. The litter box was truly disgusting and I realized I hadn't been paying enough attention to Peri's comfort.

Down on my knees, I cleaned and grovelled. "I'm really sorry, Peri. I'll get a bag of litter tomorrow on my way home from work. I promise I'll scrub and disinfect and make things nice for you. This will never happen again."

Can I have that in writing?

"Just don't ever poop on the rug, okay?"

She turned her back and flounced away.

Next evening I came home with fresh litter. She hadn't used the box or the rug during the day. When I went to the bathroom to scrub the litter box, I discovered why. She'd used the toilet.

"So how come you didn't flush?" I asked, trying to mask my excitement over her brilliance and wondering whether she'd go on using the toilet if I refused to buy cat litter.

Peri gave me a haughty look and washed a paw.

You're the slave. You flush it.

"All right," said Ben, "I get the point. If Henry is persnickety, I'll clean the box twice a day." He was still suffering from Henry's rejection of his lap and determined to do almost anything to win approval.

At home, the Houseboy put the freshly washed and filled litter box back in the laundry room and we blocked the cat door so Henry couldn't get out. Not that he'd ever used the cat door, but cat contrariness indicated he'd do so the minute we didn't want him to. I showed Henry the box. He gave it a contemptuous sniff and walked away. All right, I thought, at least he knows it's there. Several hours later, noticing his restlessness, I showed him the box again and put him in it.

He got out and shook the litter off his feet, tail twitching with indignation. The next time, I showed him how to dig in the litter and cover things with it.

You can play in this stuff if you want, but I'm having nothing to do with it.

When we went to bed that night, I was still optimistic. If we ignored his pleas to go outside, he'd be forced to use the litter box.

Morning came. Henry still hadn't used the box. He paced from door to door and window to window, demanding to go out in plaintively desperate wails. I carried him to the litter box. Several times. Each time he walked away.

Ben said, "Why don't you use the litter box yourself? Then he'd understand what it's for."

"Ben, there are limits!"

"I know lots of people who can't learn unless they're shown exactly what to do. Miss Mew must be one of those."

"I am not going to widdle in the cat's litter box. And it's 'Henry,' not 'Miss Mew.'"

"Do you think maybe Jerry doesn't know what he's doing? She's so pretty she can't possibly be male."

"He knows. You're just plain stubborn."

Some thirty-six hours after Henry came home from the hospital, he finally let loose. On the hall carpet by the front door. The new hall carpet. I knew cats had big bladders but I wasn't prepared for a flood.

He walked away, looking guilty but also annoyed that I'd forced him to do such a thing. I spent the next hour on my knees with a roll of paper towels, cloths, a bucket of water, a jug of vinegar and a garbage bag. When I thought that we could use the door without being knocked flat by the odour, I put on my jacket.

"Where are you going?" Ben asked.

"To buy Henry a cat harness," I said. "He's not going to do anything else on that carpet."

Henry did not like being fitted into his attractive red harness with its long red leash, though it looked elegant on his gray fur. I'm sure he tolerated it only because he didn't then know what it was for.

"Come on, sweetie," I said, "we're going walkies."

He was delighted to get outside, but he didn't like me trailing behind, especially when I wouldn't let him crawl under the veranda or go into a blackberry thicket. He also objected when I stopped to see what was coming up in Ben's flower garden. We cruised all over the yard, George and Nicky trotting behind with puzzled expressions. Finally Henry gave me a look of resignation and proceeded to do his business, burying it neatly afterwards, while I stared politely in the other direction.

Then he wanted to check his territory and call at the message tree, a small ornamental cedar shrub inside the front gate. I'd seen neighbourhood cats sniff around it to see who'd been there lately and spray it generously to announce they'd logged in and got their p-mail.

I let Henry leave a message at the tree but I didn't have time to help him check territory, so I headed toward the back door. George and Nicky had long since become bored with our little parade and had gone off to chase mice through the long grass and squirrels up trees. Henry followed along for maybe ten feet, then flopped on his belly. I coaxed and jiggled his lead. He refused to move. I picked him up and carried him until he struggled out of my arms. Ten feet later he flopped again.

He continued his passive resistance all the way to the back door and into the house. I shut the door, removed his lead, and went back to the hall carpet and the vinegar jug, grumbling to myself.

By the end of a week, I was getting quite good at helping Henry check territory. I was confident there'd be no more problems. Henry didn't like the leash or being taken for walks, but he grudgingly put up with it.

On the eighth day, as we were negotiating the side yard, Cal drove in, his old pickup rattling and banging. Henry turned into a windmill, wriggled out of his harness and vanished.

I nearly burst into tears. I was sure he'd never come home. He hated the harness, hated the bandage, hated going for 'walkies.' He probably hated us so much he'd adopt someone else. Somebody who wouldn't subject him to such horrible treatment. Or he'd go back to being a street cat and be run over by a car. Or his bandage would get wet and some horrible thing would happen to the wound on his leg.

Twenty minutes later, as I was pouring coffee for Cal and Ben, Henry clawed at the kitchen French doors, yelling to come in. I rushed to the door, scooped him up, cuddled him and crooned at him.

Cal looked at Ben. "What's the matter with her?"

That afternoon I tried to put his harness back on. He lowered his head and hunched his shoulders, looking remarkably like a vulture. I tried a second time.

Do that and you die!

To hell with the bandage, I thought. So let it get wet. What is to be will be.

When the time came to make an appointment with the vet to have Henry's bandage removed, I thought about the hassle of putting Henry in the cat carrier. I thought about what Jerry would say when he saw the damp, tattered, filthy bandage.

Maybe I could take the bandage off myself.

I waited until Henry was dozing in the spring sunshine by the French doors and settled beside him, scissors in hand. Cautiously I snipped through the adhesive tape and the bandage unwound itself almost without my help. Henry's leg looked healthy, though bare of fur, and the wound had healed cleanly.

Another week went by and it was time to remove the stitches. I looked at the cat carrier. Then at Henry. I decided to put off the moment for a day or two.

A friend dropped by, a doctor I'd met at drawing class in Mora Bay. I asked if she'd remove Henry's stitches.

"That would be a breach of professional ethics."

"You're joking! Just to take out three stitches?"

Sara explained at length why she couldn't remove Henry's stitches. I didn't believe a word of it; the woman was clearly afraid of my twelve-pound terrorist and his lethal-looking claws.

After she left, I looked at the stitches. They were quite dry and loose. Surely I could remove them myself?

More sun, Henry dozing, me with my trusty scissors, and the stitches came out easily. Henry purred contentedly and so did I, happy that things had worked out so well.

When Ben came in and admired my handiwork, I said, "I might train to be a veterinarian."

"Why?"

"Think of what we'd save on vet bills."

"There's a much more important reason," Ben said. "Never again would George and Henry be forced to endure the indignity of a cat cage."

"You're right; that would be worth any amount of money. Hey, I just thought of a new name for the farm. Henry's Hospital."

"Forget it," said Ben said.

"What about Sunny Acres?"

"Too trite."

"Cat Country?"

"Too cute. Sounds like a name for a store selling cat cards. Or a nation of cats."

"That's what I meant it to sound like. George the Magnificent is king of our five acres so it's his country. And I think I've figured out why he more or less invited Henry to stay and hasn't put up much fuss about Henry being in the house. He wants more subjects to boss around."

"If he wants more subjects, why didn't he let Blackjack stay?" Ben asked.

"Blackjack was our idea. I believe George thinks Henry was his idea."

***

"I have a confession to make," I said to Jerry the next time we met for bridge, this time at Jerry's and Cindy's house.

He smiled. "You removed Henry's bandage and stitches yourself."

"How did you know?"

"Well, you didn't bring him in and it's long past time for the stitches to come out. Did the wound heal cleanly?"

"It was perfect," I said. "If anything had been wrong I'd have brought him in right away. Even if getting Henry into a carrier is the worst trauma I've ever had."

Cindy laid out cards and score pads. "You should bring Ben along some evening to kibitz."

"I doubt he'd come. He's not interested in bridge and anyway, he thinks one of us should stay home to keep the animals company and let them in and out. Henry still scorns litter boxes as an invention of the devil."

"Cats have big bladders," Jerry said. "They can usually get by for at least twenty-four hours without having an accident."

"Clive's a good example of that," Cindy said. "And here he comes. I don't think you've met him before, Holly. He's usually outside pretending to be an alley cat."

Clive marched over to me, sat down with his tail curled tidily around his feet and gazed up as though ready for a long conversation. He was mostly black, his fur short and sleek. He had four neat white paws and on his chest a white dickey that came up over his mouth and nose, punctuated with a black slash like a mustache.

"Gosh, he does look like Adolph Menjou," I said.

Jerry grinned. "You're right. Acts like him, too. Every inch the gentleman."

"For sure," Cindy said. "We went to Victoria one day last month to do errands and didn't get back until early evening. Clive usually meets us at the front gate, but he didn't that day."

"He wasn't anywhere around when we went into the house, either," Jerry said.

"We'd just put our parcels down," Cindy continued, "when we heard an anguished yowl from the bedroom and I rushed to open the door. Clive raced past, giving me a sharp, short 'Merrrow!' on his way, and streaked out of the house. When I caught up, he was squatting on the nearest patch of bare earth, a look of blissful relief on his face."

"So the twenty-four hour bladder isn't necessarily true for all cats," I said.

"Oh, I think it is," Jerry said. "Clive probably slept on our bed all night. We must have shut the bedroom door on him without realizing it and we don't leave windows open when we're away for the day. So he could have been in there close to twenty-four hours."

Cindy put a plate of brownies on the sideboard. "We're just lucky he didn't decide to water any of the potted plants in the bedroom."

"Clive is certainly a gentleman," Frank said. He'd come in during the story and was on his knees scratching the cat's head. "Bring him over to meet Jezebel. I'm sure she'd be delighted to teach him the ultimate in gentlemanly behaviour: using the toilet."

XIV - THE COLONEL AND THE CORPORAL

Tom and Ginna came for Easter weekend. The first morning was sunny and redolent with the smell of new green growth and we trooped down to the beach, guarded by the two cats and Nicky, to pick over driftwood and gather clams. By afternoon, however, Tom was pacing around the yard, pretending to admire Ben's progress at staining the cedar siding forest green, but really looking for a weekend-sized construction job.

"Aren't you going to put siding on the wood shed?" Tom asked Ben.

"That's an idea. The place does look like a shack."

"No kidding! Come on, let's measure up. And this time I'll enlarge the pump house and put cedar on that, too."

I patted Ben's arm. "It's a great idea. You won't have to wriggle in there on your hands and knees next winter to prime the pump when the power goes off. And if you keep the wood shed filled, nobody will ever know what the walls looks like on the inside."

Ben gave me a mock salute. "Yessir, Madam Colonel! Next time your brother-in-law visits, I'm leaving. When the two of you get together, you turn into a pair of slave drivers. Not to mention what you do to my budget."

By dinner time, a batch of cedar siding was piled in the yard and the two men had stripped off the old weathered lumber on the pump house and were putting in footings for the new frame. Ginna and I had spent the afternoon planning the renovation of attic bedrooms and dreaming up a gourmet meal for our building crew. Compared to the frantic pace of last July's renovation, this was like being on vacation.

Later we sprawled in the living room and caught up on the news. Clyde and Jeremy had been left in Calgary with a friend of Ginna's, so the resident pets slumbered in their usual chairs, undisturbed by territorial arguments. Nicky still wanted to claim all the furniture as his, but we'd managed to restrict him to one easy chair with his own special blanket. I sat on George's favourite chair and he sat on my lap so he could be close to it.

After I told the story of how Nicky had banged his head against the blocked cat door, I said, "Did I ever tell you about the two orange tabbies I had when I lived in Vancouver?"

"No," said Tom.

"Yes," said Ben.

"No," said Ginna. "Ben, you're outvoted."

By ten we'd exhausted our repertoire of cat stories and Tom was yawning. "Come on, Ginna, let's hit the hay. I want to get some sleep before that feathered alarm clock of Ben's goes off in the morning."

High-pitched squalling woke us at midnight. Ben and I rushed out of the bedroom to find George and Henry in the hall, face to face, ears flattened, teeth bared, tails twitching, and growl-yowling, as cats do when they're threatening to kill each other. George was trying to evict Henry. Henry said he had as much right to live in this house as anybody else and he wasn't leaving. Nicky stood a safe distance away and whined.

This was something new. Henry had always yielded to George's wishes and superior status. His happy-go-lucky nature didn't lend itself to palace intrigue and he'd made it clear he was no threat to George's sovereignty.

We separated them before they damaged each other and I put Henry in my studio. Ben shut George in his den, had his arm clawed in the process and swore loudly.

"We must have paid too much attention to Henry after his operation," Ben said. "It's obvious George has decided Something Must Be Done."

"So he's decreed Henry will have to go. Well, I'm not letting George win this one. I'll invoke the War Measures Act and assert my latent authority as Head Cat."

"George is being ridiculous; Henry's a member of the family," said the Houseboy, as he mopped the blood off his scratches and handed me the Band Aids. "If you're going head to head with His Majesty, you'd better wear elbow- length leather gloves. He's very upset."

George wasn't the only one.

Ben went back to bed but I paced the rest of the night, sick at heart. I told myself not to worry but I couldn't help it. Nicky paced with me for a while, nuzzling at my hand as though he knew I was unhappy, but eventually got fed up and went back to bed, too. In spite of my brave words about being Head Cat, I knew George would never give in. But I couldn't allow Henry to be kicked out.

One of them would have to go to the SPCA. Which one? I couldn't bear the thought of either of them leaving. He might be adopted by someone cruel. Or he'd be put down. I crushed the tranquillizers left over from our bout with Henry and the cat carrier, nursing some vague idea of keeping both of them in permanent la-la land.

At seven I decided there was only one thing to do. It probably wouldn't work but I had to give them another chance. Apprehensive, I opened the doors to both rooms. George and Henry met in the hallway, gave each other a friendly sniff, marched into the kitchen and sat side by side at the feeding station. I was so relieved that I cursed both of them in English, my night school Spanish and a few words I made up on the spot. I told them they didn't deserve food, then opened a can of the most expensive tuna we had.

At breakfast, Ben said, "Now that I know cats so much better, I'm seeing a lot of similarities to humans." He shook pepper on his hash browns. "I've come up with nicknames for our two according to military rank. George is The Colonel and Henry is The Corporal."

At that moment Henry made the mistake of infringing on George's personal space at the French doors and got a smack on the head. George marched through the kitchen toward the cat door, Henry trotting along behind.

"See?" Ben said. "George metes out punishment and never smiles. Henry allows George to precede him through doorways and backs down the moment George raises a paw."

Pleased with Ben's conversion to cat-watcher, I got into the spirit of the game. "And in civilian life, George wears a tie and tails, sips martinis and uses a cigarette holder. Henry wears a torn T-shirt and baseball cap and slurps beer right out of the can."

"I'd call them Patrician and Peasant," Ginna said. "That fits with how they were sleeping in the living room last night. George had his tail, paws and head tucked in neatly and looked like a perfectly round ball of fur. Henry had his head hanging off the edge of the pillow and his legs were sticking out in every direction. He looked as though someone had tossed him there when he was drunk and he still hadn't sobered up."

I liked Ginna's idea. Patrician George had delicate legs, a svelte body and tiny feet, and carried his head proudly and his body erect like a true aristocrat. Peasant Henry had stocky legs, big feet and long, messy hair and tripped over the carpet. When he chased a string, he didn't snatch it out of mid-air with precision, as George did; he trampled it to death.

"How about Batman and Robin?" Tom drained his coffee mug. "George leaps tall buildings in a single bound."

"You mean refrigerators and upright pianos," I said.

"Ginna's idea is closer to the truth," Ben said. "You should watch George on the open shelves in the dining room. He parades around among all the knickknacks and delicate china and never knocks anything over."

"Henry goes to sleep on the back of the couch," I said, "and falls onto the floor behind it. He staggers out, eyes half-shut, fur ruffled, and clambers back to his perch, wondering how it got away from him."

Ben poured second mugs of coffee. "I still like Colonel and Corporal best. George bellows loud, imperious orders and, if we don't obey instantly, he lectures us just the way officers lecture men on the parade ground."

"That's right," I said. "Henry, on the other hand, never lectures, never demands. He waits patiently until I notice him, or says 'Prrrt', which sounds like a purr and a meow together. Then he leads me to the door or the food can he wants opened."

Tom said, "And I suppose you're so grateful not to be yelled at that you do everything he wants."

"How did you guess?"

"Because Clyde and Jeremy operate much the same way. I think Henry knows exactly how to handle you."

"If George and Henry are The Colonel and The Corporal," Ginna said, "then what is Nicky?"

At the sound of his name, Nicky got up, wagging his tail, put his chin on Ginna's lap and gave her a soulful look. She buried her hands in his thick white fur, then caressed his softly pointed ears. "You're adorable," she said. "Maybe you don't need to be anything but a dog."

"There's only one thing he can be." I said. "Both cats order him around, so he has to be The Private."

***

While I stirred clam chowder for lunch and Ginna made garlic bread, it occurred to me that the Colonel and the Corporal might be very different but they also had several things in common. Other than both having me under their paws, that is.

George liked to lie on the Houseboy's newspaper. Since the editorial page was as necessary as breathing for Ben, I admired the way he denied himself until George decided to move. Henry thought my crossword puzzles were meant for him to sleep on.

"That explains why we never seem to finish the morning paper until late at night," I said to Ginna.

"Clyde and Jeremy hate noise," Ginna said. "How about your two?"

"Well, George reacts to the vacuum cleaner with the same revulsion that Ben has for rock music. But Henry opens one eye as the cleaner passes and goes back to sleep."

"What happens when you play the piano?"

"George yowls like a saber-toothed tiger, paces, and tries to push me off the piano stool. Henry sits looking up at me with such an agonized, pleading expression that I worry about the music hurting his ears."

"How about Nicky?"

"He barks at the door until somebody lets him out."

We were still talking about cat foibles when Ben and Tom came in for lunch.

"Don't you two ever think about anything but cats and food?" Tom asked.

"What else is there?" Ginna asked in mock amazement.

"Hard-working hungry men. Is that clam chowder I smell?" Tom peered over my shoulder as I reached into the fridge. "What are those little green things in the bowl?"

"Eggs," I said. "Araucana eggs."

"They look revolting."

"Once you get the shell off, they look and taste like ordinary eggs," I said.

"Maybe so, but I'm not eating them."

"Where's your sense of adventure?"

"He never has adventures with food," Ginna said, "only with hammers and saws."

I poured the unadventurous chowder into bowls and we sat down. George and Henry lay in front of the French doors, alert for any bits of clam that might come their way.

"The Colonel and the Corporal work hard, too," Ben said. "You see what they're doing now?"

"They're stretched out on the floor, relaxing."

"You're misinterpreting outward appearances. In fact, they're preventing the sun from fading the new tiles. In a perfect world, they'd be resting instead."

"Just like Jeremy." Ginna picked up her spoon. "He lies on the clean laundry so no one will steal it."

"What dedication!" Ben said. "Holly, aren't you ashamed that you haven't noticed these wonderful qualities before? And you call yourself a Cat Person!"

When I lay down for a nap that afternoon, I noted that the royals had yet another thing in common; they both liked kneading. Henry plumped down on my chest, his back to me, and pushed his paws against my tummy as though it were bread dough, kneading himself into a trance. It seemed an effective way of meditating and I got drowsy watching him in spite of the occasional claw piercing my shirt. George sat on my thighs, kneading hard enough to insert the tips of all his claws into my skin. Finally I rose, much faster than a loaf of bread, and went to the bathroom to fetch the nail clippers.

George let me clip his claws without any fuss, which was unusual. Often the job required two people, one to hold him still and one to clip. But Henry, when I reached for one of his paws, hunched his shoulders, lowered his head and did his vulture act.

Not wishing to deal with a mutiny, I put the clippers away and curled up on the bed again. I was happy to go along with Henry's philosophy of 'live and let live' but I pulled a blanket over me in case he decided to have another kneading and meditation session.

XV - THE KING'S APPRENTICE

April slid into May and Ben worked long days in the vegetable garden. I rebelled against my brown thumb status and planted sweet peas along the front of the veranda and tacked netting to the rails for them to climb. Nicky, now almost full grown, followed us everywhere. So did the cats. All three were fascinated by our habit of burying things in the ground and occasionally dug the seeds up again to see what they were.

When Ben swore at them, I said, "They're only trying to help. Sometimes they put fertilizer in with the seed and bury it again."

"Well, I wish they'd stop. Steer manure is the only proper dressing for gardens."

George picked his own spring task, which was to indoctrinate Henry into the ways of royalty. George did not hold with torn T-shirts, drinking beer from the bottle, or laissez-faire attitudes. Cats were superior beings, George most superior of all. He would teach Henry to give up his peasant ways.

The first thing George demonstrated was upchucking. Henry watched the performance and wandered away, bored. Next day, apparently spurred by the King's enthusiasm, he gave it a try.

When it was over, Henry had decided upchucking was a phenomenon visited on him by dark powers and, fortunately for our sanity and carpets, his first time was his last. When his stomach began to heave, he looked terrified and tried to outrun the evil thing. With each spasm, he leapt three feet and ran ten, throwing up as he went. By the time he'd decorated the living room, the kitchen, the hall and Ben's den, he'd accomplished more in one minute than George ever had with his carefully orchestrated three upchucks during breakfast.

I felt so sorry for Henry that I couldn't get angry about cleaning up after him.

"If George learned to look pathetic instead of arrogant," I said, "he'd have a more appreciative audience."

"It won't ever happen," Ben said. "George would rather give up all nine lives than look like a wimp."

He wouldn't accept failure either. If Henry couldn't be taught to throw up, he could certainly learn to be finicky about food and water.

In this Henry was a credit to his teacher and the two of them worked out a routine that drove us crazy. Henry knew George's food tasted better than his, and George was just as sure Henry had the better deal, though they were eating exactly the same thing. When they decided their own food was acceptable after all, George wouldn't eat his because Henry had contaminated it with his peasant tongue. Henry wouldn't eat his because he was full of George's. Nicky gulped down the leftovers. Ten minutes later George would be back, demanding more food.

George regarded having Ben feed him at the table as his exclusive privilege, however. When Henry and Nicky demanded equal rights and I fed them bits off my plate, George acted like a fur-covered vacuum cleaner and ate their portions as well as his own. Tired of watching pieces of chicken disappear from under their noses, they'd return to their dry kibble in the kitchen, selflessly saving George from overindulgence and indigestion.

One day I sat at the kitchen table to eat a slice of freshly baked bread. Henry stared at it disappearing into my mouth, his slanted yellow eyes full of yearning.

"Want some, Henry?" If George turned up his nose at broccoli, surely Henry would hate unbuttered bread. I handed him a tiny piece. He ate it with obvious pleasure and nuzzled my hand, asking for more.

George may have approved Henry's eccentricity, but he disdained the bread – after checking to make sure he wasn't missing anything. It was fun feeding Henry because he was so good-natured and I assumed he'd be happy to eat bread any time I offered it to him. I should have known better. Some days he liked bread; some days he didn't.

When I complained to Ben, he said, "You should thank those cats for making your life interesting."

"I could stand a little boredom. Including cats who eat what we give them and shut up about it."

Having achieved success with food, George moved on to water. Although the water in his bathroom water dish was replaced every day, he often preferred a muddy pool in a low, wet corner of the orchard. Bark, leaves and dead spiders must have given the water a rich, unique flavour.

As far as Henry was concerned, if it hadn't fallen out of the sky it wasn't water and he wasn't going to drink it. With one exception; when one of us had a shower, he'd climb into the bathtub to lick up the droplets of water.

"I suppose the shower sounds like rain to him," I said to Ben. "I'm all in favour. If Henry licks the tub clean, that's less housework for me to do."

"But the soap scum can't be good for his system."

"If Henry likes it, then it must fulfill some deep primeval need in him."

Henry's preferred source of water, other than stagnant pools, was the veranda, where the plank flooring was so warped it collected rain in shallow pools. I got tired of drying off his long, thick fur when he insisted on going out to drink for five minutes in a driving rain storm, and fed up with pouring water on the deck for him during dry spells. I didn't mind doing it when he actually drank, but half the time he stared at me as if I was out of my mind. It was hard not to agree with him.

"Supposing," I said to Ben, "that I buy a shallow dish, the same green as the paint on the veranda? If I put that next to his food dish and make sure he watches me pouring water into it, maybe he'll think that's okay."

Henry scorned the green plastic dish. One day I found him drinking from the metal watering can Ben kept outside for filling up the chickens' water dish. Next day both cats drank from it, standing on their hind legs and sticking their heads underneath the handle to get at the rusty water.

I experimented with a plastic watering bucket on the step outside the kitchen and, amazingly, both George and Henry deigned to drink out of it. Encouraged, I put an identical container of water on the kitchen floor, mirroring the container on the other side of the sliding glass door which we'd installed to replace the French doors.

Both cats drank from that, too. Sometimes. But they still preferred stale puddles of water in the orchard. Nicky's favourite drinking water was out of the toilet. We tried to solve that by keeping the lid down, but he soon learned to flip it up with his nose.

"Those royals may appreciate gourmet food but when it comes to the wine list, they have no palate whatsoever," I said to Ben.

"You just don't appreciate the subtle nuances of properly aged water."

***

My early morning peregrinations usually took me to my studio, where I'd drink my first coffee and let ideas for stories and poems roll around in my mind. One morning in mid-May, I headed for the veranda instead. As I stepped out, I saw four deer grazing in Ben's garden. Oddly, they were in a small group rather than spread out among the rows.

The reason soon became obvious. One deer moved toward the far end of the garden. Nicky appeared from behind the group, galloped after it and herded it back with its mates.

"Nicky! You're supposed to chase them, not herd them." He ignored me — had he learned that from George? — and I chased the deer away myself. Nicky helped, but tried to round up the deer as they moved across the meadow.

At least the deer would keep him occupied and at home for an hour or so. Ben's 'guard' dog was everyone's friend and he often tried to go off with people who came to buy eggs, or went visiting on his own. Looking for him had introduced us to many of our neighbours.

When Ben woke, I described Nicky's herding efforts. "I think you'll need to build a deer-proof fence after all."

Ben groaned. "I'm not giving in yet. There has to be another way." He walked to the window and peered out at the blue sky. "I'm going to get the pool ready today. It's definitely swimming weather."

I poured coffee. "If you sold some of the pool components, that would pay for part of a new fence. Might even pay for all of it."

"We may as well wait until fall," Ben said.

I suppressed a sigh. If we had a hot summer, Ben would be more than ever in love with that pool and I'd never be able to talk him into getting rid of it.

Cal came over for coffee midmorning and laughed when he heard about Nicky's efforts to help the deer demolish the garden one row at a time.

"It's a good thing they have other farms to visit," I said. "If ours was the only garden available to them, it would be wiped out by now."

"Maybe you should think about raising deer instead of chickens. There's a good market for venison." Cal peered at the bowl I'd taken from the fridge. "Those funny little green eggs from the Araucanas?"

"Yes and I think we're going to let them raise chicks for awhile instead of searching for their eggs every morning. They lay eggs under the blackberry bushes, in the orchard and I wouldn't be surprised if they sneak off down to the forest. They don't take to regimentation and nest boxes at all."

"They're kinda cute, though," Cal said.

***

George thought Henry's worst fault was his failure to take hunting seriously. This frustrated the King but endeared Henry to Ben, who was fond of watching the birds eating at his feeders and splashing in the bird bath.

One afternoon we watched George handle a training session. Having told Henry to sit on the veranda and observe, George was belly down in the grass, absolutely still, waiting for a small bird to move a foot closer. Henry soon became bored. His ears perked forward, he marched off the veranda and over to George, eyeing him curiously.

Wotcha doin', George?

Every bird in the yard flew away. George rose to his feet, ears back, and walked wearily back to the veranda, muttering about stupid cats who didn't understand the thrill of the chase. He became more determined than ever to teach Henry that all cats, especially royal cats, find great pleasure in hunting and stalking.

George caught two birds the next day and brought them into the house as offerings, Henry trotting behind on both occasions. The first bird was still alive and I managed to set it free. The second gave one last twitch and died as George dropped it at my feet.

Henry sniffed the bird with an expression of disgust, then walked away, the arch of his back and the angle of his tail clearly expressing contempt.

Later, as I stood at the kitchen counter, a raucous but strangely muffled yowl announced Henry's presence. I turned to see what he wanted.

Henry tossed the dried skeleton of a long-dead bird, a few feathers still attached, at my feet. He walked away, feathery tail waving triumphantly.

"Henry's an intellectual," I said to Ben. "He was teaching us that such triumphs are short-lived."

"These cats have too darn much personality." He threw the skeleton into the garbage can.

George finally gave up on teaching Henry to hunt, but he seemed to think he had to make up for Henry's deficiency by catching twice as many creatures.

One morning George chased a gray squirrel across the yard and up the tall Garry oak which grew next to a grove of arbutus and fir beyond the orchard. The rough, ridged bark of the oak's spreading branches was ideal for climbing, but George didn't follow at once. About twenty feet up, the squirrel turned around and swore loudly at George, its bushy tail flicking rapidly.

The verbal trouncing didn't bother George. He stood at the foot of the tree, his own tail lashing, about to climb up after the squirrel. He'd seen a thousand squirrels skittering from branch to branch and tree to tree, almost as agile as birds, but George was a perpetual optimist. One of these days a really clumsy squirrel would come along.

Two crows, who had nestlings in a neighbouring arbutus, started dive bombing the squirrel. It came a little way down the tree, swearing at everybody, took another look at George and went back up again. The crows intensified their intimidation tactics. The squirrel held its ground, yelling defiantly in both directions.

The crows became bolder and the squirrel had to make a decision. It raced down the tree and jumped, landing a foot in front of George's face. I held my breath, sure George would pounce. Henry and Nicky sat twenty feet away, like spectators at the games in an ancient Roman amphitheatre. It was hard to tell whether they were rooting for George or the squirrel.

George, startled by the squirrel's insolence, leapt backwards. The squirrel made a fast U-turn and streaked for another tree. By the time George recovered his aplomb, the squirrel had raced through the tree-tops, then down into the blackberry brambles on Cal's side of the fence, well away from both cat and crows.

Pretending indifference, George sat down and leisurely washed his face, then daintily picked his way across the grass to the house. The King might have been an optimist about squirrels, but he knew when to quit.

"I'm surprised Henry isn't keen on hunting," Ben said. "I thought all cats were avid hunters."

"Are all men avid hunters?"

"Well, no, but..."

"I think we'll just have to accept that Henry is a Buddhist at heart and be thankful. Perhaps we should get a cat that George can train properly."

"We don't need any more personalities in this house. I've got all I can do to keep up with George and Henry."

XVI - CANDIDATES FOR THE COUCH

It was late May and time to celebrate Ben's birthday again. I couldn't believe the year had gone by so quickly. As I iced his cake, I realized we'd been on the farm fifteen months. Only nine more until Ben and I sat down to review our agreement and I could return to the city I loved, to my old friends and my bridge group. It wasn't that I couldn't stand living on the farm, but I knew I'd be much happier in Victoria. Besides, if Ben didn't stop being so stubborn about building a deer fence around the garden, he'd never make a success of market gardening anyway.

"Those cats are crazy," Ben said, coming into the kitchen with the morning egg collection. "They won't eat the T-bone steak I cut up for their breakfast. And why would Henry choose to sleep on the kitchen table last night when there are so many softer beds in the house?"

"That's not very weird. But I have known cats that could do with a session on a psychiatrist's couch. Did I ever tell you about Anna the Siamese?"

"Yes, you have." He put the eggs into the fridge and poured himself a coffee.

"I don't think I told you this story."

Anna had never been outside my apartment. When I moved to a house I thought she'd be happy to go out and explore the yard. Not so. The moment her feet touched the grass she yowled and leapt onto my shoulder. Never again would she go outside unless she was draped around my neck.

"That is weird," Ben said. "I thought all cats liked the outdoors and chasing birds."

"You know Henry doesn't chase birds."

"Yes, but he's different."

"You used to think cats were all alike. And boring."

"I know." Ben took a date square out of the fridge to go with his coffee. "You don't have to remind me. Now I'm probably more of a sucker for them then you are."

"I wonder how Nicky and Beanbag will get along." Ben's son Gareth, his wife Sue and their corgi were coming for the weekend to help Ben eat his birthday cake.

"Like a house on fire. Dogs don't fight." At the sound of tires crunching on gravel, Ben got up and peered out the window over the sink. "Oops, it's Hilda coming to buy eggs. I'm outta here."

I felt the same way; Hilda barely stopped talking long enough to draw breath. But when you're an Egg Lady, you have to be nice to the customers. I opened the back door.

A white toy poodle stood beside Hilda. "This is Mitzi. I usually leave her in the car, but I was hoping you'd offer me some coffee today. I want to tell you about the quilting group I'm planning to start this fall."

"I'd be happy to have a coffee with you, but Mitzi should stay in your car. I have two cats in the house."

"Don't worry," she said, "Mitzi won't hurt your cats."

"It's not my cats I'm worried about."

Hilda laughed and came in with her empty egg cartons. Mitzi smelled the tantalizing odour of cat and skittered across the tile floor in search of it. When she trotted into the living room, I followed her because I knew George and Henry were snoozing on the couch.

George, blinking sleep out of his eyes, stood up, his back arched like a Halloween cat. Mitzi went into a frenzy of yapping. Henry yawned.

George gathered himself into attack mode, a gleeful look on his face. Finally! A dog my own size.

He launched himself at the poodle. I grabbed him just as he got his claws in and Mitzi fled, yelping, back to her mistress.

"Well, really," Hilda said, cuddling a still quivering Mitzi in her arms. "Poor little sweetheart. Cats are such spineless creatures as a rule; I had no idea one would dare attack a dog. There, there, sweetheart, did the nasty old cat frighten you?"

Hilda drank her coffee quickly and I declined, with pleasure, her invitation to join the quilting group.

Gareth and company arrived mid-evening. After Nicky and Beanbag did their ritual sniffing and posturing and decided they liked each other, we admired Ben's garden, flower beds and the hanging baskets on the veranda.

"They're gorgeous," Sue said, "except for that one at the end. Why does it look so wilted?"

"There's a family of finches nesting in it." Ben carefully lifted down the basket and four baby finches blinked at us from among the geranium stalks.

"They're cute," Sue said, "even if their beaks do look bigger than their bodies. Why didn't you move the nest?"

"Didn't want to disturb them." Ben hung the basket up again. "I can't water the plants, in case the babies get wet, but they'll be grown up and gone soon."

At dusk we settled in for a good gossip. Beanbag lay at Gareth's feet and Nicky lay beside Ben, his hero. George eyed Beanbag speculatively from Ben's chair but he'd already had his fun with Mitzi. He put his head on his paws and went back to sleep. Henry came down from his perch on the window sill and wandered toward the corgi.

"Henry, come here," I said. "Don't frighten the dog."

Henry sat down two feet away from Beanbag and stared. The corgi looked worried. Henry flopped down on his back and waved his paws around.

"He wants to play," I said.

When Beanbag didn't move, Henry gave up. He hopped up on the couch, sprawled in Sue's lap and purred at her.

"We found out why Beanbag is afraid of cats." Sue stroked Henry and he gazed up at her adoringly.

Gareth said, "His previous owners told us he was out in their back yard one day when a big gray and white tabby attacked him. The tabby jumped on Beanbag's back, stuck his claws in and rode him all over the yard. Beanbag finally scraped him off by crawling under the back porch."

"Poor old mutt," Ben said, giving the dog a scratch behind the ears. "Holly says George attacked a toy poodle this morning."

"That's because the poodle was small enough for him to handle," I said. "George is a noble creature, after all. His inbred sense of fair play dictates that he spar only with an animal his own size."

"If you're going to talk rot, I'm going to pour everybody a drink," Ben said.

***

We'd talked of going to Mora Bay for the birthday dinner but the others decided it would be more relaxing to have it at home. It would be more work for me, but George and Henry were pleased. They knew, when they saw us changing our 'fur', that we were going out and took offense at being left all alone. Not that they would be lonely with two dogs to tease, but the furniture might take a beating in the process.

Sue was watching me stir gravy when I stepped back and tripped over Henry. The spoon hit the floor, spattering gravy, and Henry gave me a short sharp lecture before flouncing off.

"You'd think that cat would know by now that I can move in reverse," I said, as I mopped up the spattered gravy.

"Of course he knows," Sue said. "But he hadn't given you permission to move." For a woman who'd had only dogs as pets, she was catching on quickly.

"Or he thinks I have eyes in my heels. Cats are weird."

"I bet they think we're even weirder."

"You're probably right," I said, wondering if Sue might turn out to be a Cat Person. "When they bring me a bird or a mouse, I lose it. I'm too clumsy to climb trees and to stupid to roll in the catnip. When I go outside they follow me until I'm safely back in the house."

Ben came into the kitchen to check on the roast beef. Gareth followed, saw Henry sitting on the kitchen table, supervising, and cried, "Hey, there's a cat on the table!"

"Oh, dear!" the Houseboy said, and quickly removed Henry, who blinked in utter disbelief. He'd been kicked off editorials before, but never the kitchen table.

Ben and Gareth went back to the living room and Henry returned to his post. I poured Sue a glass of wine and began chopping vegetables for the salad.

"We put in a new furnace a couple of months ago," I said, "and that experience proved cats think humans are crazy. Or stupid. When the heat came on, the cold air returns howled like a January gale. The first time it happened, Henry headed for the door, wailing."

"Poor baby," Sue said, stroking him.

"I petted him and told him I wasn't frightened. But he was convinced something was wrong and I was too stupid to realize it. It took three weeks for him to decide the noise was harmless, but meanwhile, every time the heat came on he yelled at me to go outside with him where it was safe."

"Was George frightened, too?"

"George? Never! He knows nothing in the house would dare hurt him. All he did was glare at the cold air return and go back to sleep."

After dinner, we lazed in the living room, too full to do anything, including the dishes. Ben was working on his second brandy when George climbed up on his chest, stared him in the eye and bellowed.

"What does he want?" Sue asked.

"His ruff." Ben got up, sighing.

Gareth said, "What's a 'ruff'?"

I answered because the Houseboy was now following George down the hall. "A body massage. George demands at least two per day, more if he can talk Ben into it."

"I take it there's a little ritual?" Sue asked.

"Oh, indeed! The procedure is for Ben to take George to his den, kneel on the floor and gently massage His Imperial Fussiness all over."

"Dad does this every day?" Gareth asked. "Sounds like George is as demanding as Beanbag. After all the insulting things my father has said about cats, it's hard to believe he's letting his life be run by two of them."

"A ten-pound cat can wield a lot of power."

Beanbag put his head on Gareth's knee and gave him an imploring look. "As much as a forty-pound animated sausage, I guess."

A few moments later Ben, with George marching at his heels, came back to his chair and brandy. George sat down, stared at him intently and meowed.

"Forget it, your Majesty! That's the third ruff today. You've had more than your share."

George looked at me.

"No way! I gave you a ten-minute brushing today." In April I'd bought a cat brush and given him a going-over with it. The procedure had instantly become an unbreakable thousand-year-old tradition. So far I'd successfully fought off his attempts to make me do it twice a day.

George eyed Ben again, then walked over to one of the stereo speakers and inserted his front claws into it.

Ben and I simultaneously screamed "George!" and leapt for him but, as usual, he eluded us, scooting through the dining room and into the kitchen with his ears back and tail lashing.

"Can't you break him of that?" Gareth asked.

I gave Gareth and Sue several examples of why it was impossible to train George not to do exactly what he wanted to do whenever he wanted to do it. "Anyway, the material used for those speaker covers is too strong for him to destroy. The threads are pulled out a tiny bit where George puts his claws in, but they don't break. I bet you didn't even notice the nubbly effect."

Gareth admitted that he hadn't.

"We do clip his claws, but this house will have to be advertised as a 'handyman special' if we ever decide to sell," Ben said.

"They don't mean to do any damage." I pointed at the piano. "See the evenly spaced claw marks? Those were caused by George escaping from a playful Henry."

We went upstairs and I showed them the second spare bedroom wallpaper, hanging in tatters on either side of the bed. "Before Ben built the scratching post, George used to scratch that to tell me he was hungry, thirsty, or wanted butler service. Like an order pad, I guess."

"Or," Sue said, "maybe just because it seemed like a great idea at the time."

I could definitely see a Cat Person lurking under that blonde hair and in those dog-habituated hands.

"I suggested papering the room with steel plate in an interesting shade of gray but Ben said the walls would sink into the crawl space and there was no point aggravating the situation."

Downstairs, Gareth suggested hanging the stereo speakers on the wall.

"They'd just pick some other way of attracting my attention," I said. "They don't use the speakers to sharpen their claws – they have a scratching post for that. And they don't scratch the wallpaper upstairs any more because we're sleeping downstairs now."

"At least you can keep the hair vacuumed up," Sue said.

"You mean I should be thankful for small mercies? All right, but what am I going to do about the stacked plastic filing trays in my den?"

Weeks before, Henry had taken to sleeping on the top one and it cracked. Ben mended it with a glue reputed to weld steel to steel successfully. Henry climbed on for a nap and the tray broke again. Ben next glued a sheet of thin plywood to the floor of the tray. That, too, cracked under Henry's weight. Ben topped the plywood with more plywood. Henry went aboard, thumped down and the tray broke for the fourth time.

Gareth said, "Why not buy new trays?"

"Fixing them is a challenge," Ben said. "I just have to figure out how. In the meantime, we follow the principle of propping things up with other things, the way they used to do it in early Gothic cathedrals."

"That principle really came in handy when one of the back legs on the couch fell off," I said. "We put two cans of stewed tomatoes under that corner. As long as nobody bounces on the couch, it works just fine."

I took Gareth and Sue into my studio and showed them the stacks of paperbacks separating the three trays. "This works well, too. Henry couldn't possibly break a tray now. Of course, I can't file anything in them."

Sue grinned. "A small price to pay for the happiness of a fat, good-natured cat."

Gareth snorted. "I'm going to go drink brandy with my father."

"I'll bet Henry hasn't slept up there since you did that," Sue guessed.

"You're right. But if I take the books away, he's sure to come back. Then George will follow and start sleeping in the filing cabinet again. He's already shed hair into my files and kicked over the box of floppy disks."

"Why don't you keep the file drawers shut?"

"Because I'm always reaching in to grab a different disk or another file."

"How about keeping your studio door shut?"

"When I do that, they sit outside and yowl. Or scratch the door."

Sue laughed and shook her head. "I'm not sure I'd want to live with your two babies. Beanbag can be a nuisance but he's not that bad."

"I'd never give them up," I said. "They're too much fun, in spite of the mess they make."

"I can suggest a different attitude. Pretend they're great artists, avant-garde deconstructionists."

"What does that mean?"

"In literature, deconstruction means to take each sentence apart and analyse the words in terms of culture. George and Henry are merely taking your house and furniture apart and analysing them to determine what kind of culture humans have."

"And I should rejoice in being a handmaiden to genius?"

"Something like that."

"I think I'd rather have a brandy."

"I'll have wine." As she turned toward the door, Sue saw the jade plant she'd given me. "Oh, Holly, you really do have a brown thumb, don't you? Would you mind if I take this poor little plant home and nurse it back to health?"

"Not at all. And don't give it back to me; you can see what will happen if you do."

Pouring drinks in the kitchen, I said, "Nicky doesn't get into much trouble. Are all dogs easy to live with?"

"No. Beanbag drives me crazy sometimes."

"Do you suppose we're masochists?"

"I hate to think so," Sue said, "but what other explanation can there be?"

"I don't know, but I prefer being called a handmaiden to genius."

We spent the rest of the evening by the fire, petting lap-cats and scratching dogs' ears. The conversation ranged from politics to cats to computers to cats to market gardening and back to cats again. At midnight, after Gareth suggested calling the farm 'Cat City' and Ben groaned, Sue and Gareth headed upstairs to bed.

As I turned off the lights in the living room, I heard Gareth say, "They really do have two tins of stewed tomatoes holding up one corner of the couch. I looked. I wonder why they don't get it fixed properly."

"They're living on an island," Sue said, her voice fading up the stairs, "They're supposed to be eccentric."

"They were eccentric before they ever moved here. My father probably has his budget drawn up for the next year and didn't put in anything for furniture repair. Knowing him, that means the stewed tomatoes stay where they are until he does a new one."

XVII - LESE FELINITY

The hot days of summer had Ben worried about the well going dry again and muttering about water for the garden. When I suggested doing a rain dance, he gave me a dirty look. I went off to my den and wrote a new short story, though the first two were still bouncing back with the persistence of moths against a lit window. I shut the royals out of my studio one afternoon so I could concentrate on finishing it. They were not impressed when I said I was sacrificing the pleasure of their company for my art and scratched at the door until I let them in again. Ben told me I'd committed lese felinity, akin to lese majesty, offending the power and dignity of the king.

"What about the offenses those two commit against my person, property and sanity?" I asked.

"You know there's no justice for slaves. Their Highnesses consider it sufficient that you have a warm bed and enough to eat. Where's your gratitude, woman? Why do I always have to remind you how lucky you are?"

George suffered many offenses against his power and dignity. That evening, for example, Ben sat in his easy chair and opened a new library book. George immediately sat on the book, his front paws on the Houseboy's chest. When Ben didn't respond with a two-handed pet, George gently inserted his needle-sharp claws into Ben's chest.

"Ouch! Don't do that!" Ben put George on the arm of the chair, patted him, and picked up the book again.

They repeated this routine again. And again. After five minutes Ben committed lese felinity by putting George on the floor. The King sat with his back to the Houseboy, ears back, scowling.

"I'm sorry, George, but I've had enough. You can come back up if you behave yourself."

George flicked his tail again. *If WHO behaves himself? This slave had better watch it or he'll end up in the arena with half a dozen lions circling him.*

I was on the couch with a coffee and my knitting. George curled up in my lap, flicking his ears in irritation when the strand of wool tickled them. Henry, sprawling on the back of the couch, decided to get in on the act. He started walking down my front, but there wasn't room to lie beside George, so he stayed where he was, hind feet on my shoulder, front feet on my stomach, and went into a coma.

Normally I enjoyed the attention. On this occasion I committed lese felinity by announcing firmly that I had to go out to the kitchen to turn the pork chops and everyone would have to move now, please.

I tried to atone that night, my back propped against the bed headboard, my usual cup of tea, handful of grapes, chunk of cheese and murder mystery in hand. Henry turned circles on my chest and stomach, occasionally stopping to knead, while George nuzzled my hand for little bits of cheese and Ben told me long complex theories about fertilizing gardens and building greenhouses. Though all these demands made it difficult to read, drink and eat, I didn't complain nearly as much as I wanted to.

Then Henry thumped my forehead with his in affectionate greeting and got nose prints on my glasses so I decided to give up my selfish pursuits and go to sleep. But how could I? There were two cats curled up on my body and I'd be committing lese felinity by moving. I managed to wriggle out of my dressing gown, toss my extra pillow and the book on the floor, put my glasses and the grape dish on the bedside table and turn out the lamp without disturbing the royals. The hard part, as always, was squirming toward the foot of the bed so I could eventually rest my head on a pillow. At the moment of success, the royals, fed up with their heaving mattress, jumped off the bed and headed for the living room.

Henry, these servants are hopeless.

Could we trade them in, Your Highness?

The new ones might be worse.

Ben liked to sleep in on Sunday, but the cats rose with the dawn, no matter the day. They wanted their breakfast at once and, of course, nagged me instead of Ben. I didn't mind; I liked watching the sun rise. After the fur brigade had been fed and George and Nicky had gone back to sleep, I sat on the veranda with a coffee. Henry stretched out beside my chair, his chin resting on his front paws and watched the morning with as much interest as I did.

His philosophy of 'live and let live' intrigued me. I'd never known a cat so unconcerned with privilege and territory. All cats live in the moment but Henry seemed to make it a special quality. As I was musing on this phenomenon, I saw an adult rabbit hunkered down on the meadow edge of the lawn. Then a half-grown squirrel came down the old Garry oak near the fence and bounced across to the rabbit. The rabbit ran to the swimming pool, stopped and looked back.

"Surely," I said to Henry, who was sitting up now, ears perked forward, "that rabbit can't be afraid of an animal so much smaller than itself."

The squirrel raced after the rabbit, turning a couple of somersaults on the way. The rabbit let it get within a couple of feet, then ran back across the lawn.

And the game was on. The rabbit let the squirrel chase him round and round the yard, zigging and zagging. When they met face to face, the squirrel jumped over the rabbit and kept on going. They continued their game of tag for another five minutes, while Henry and I lazed on the deck. The game seemed to amuse him as much as it did me.

Nicky wandered out and flopped next to Henry, who sat up and licked the dog's face, then worked on the inside of one ear. Nicky stood the tickling for only a moment before he lifted a big paw and pinned Henry to the deck. Henry squirmed, then put his head down and fell asleep. If that had been George, I thought, he'd have been yowling about lese felinity. But the King, always conscious of his superior status, would never have lowered himself to washing the dog's face.

Later that morning I looked out the laundry room window and saw an adult squirrel playing with Henry on the driveway. The squirrel danced back and forth, barely a foot from Henry's nose, flicked its tail and dashed away. Henry, his plume of a gray tail straight up, ears forward, trotted after it. When the squirrel approached again, Henry sat down and gazed with rapt attention at the saucy little creature. They repeated the manoeuver several times before the mailman startled them and the squirrel vanished into the orchard.

Perhaps wild animals, as well as tame, sense when another animal is prepared to mind his own business and forego aggression. The Mighty Hunter, had he been around to observe the incident, would have been appalled at Henry's lack of enterprise. Yet it had been George's idea to adopt Henry as one of his subjects and the King had mellowed since Henry brought his easy-going attitudes to the kingdom. Even Ben had become so mellow he was putty in the paws of both cats and I suppose I wasn't far behind. I decided I would try to write a poem about Henry and his Buddhist attitude.

I told Ben about Henry and the squirrel and said, "One can't commit lese felinity against Henry because he doesn't think he owns the world. But Peri was more like George, quick to take insult."

"Not another Peri story!"

"She went after a bird sitting on the ledge outside my apartment window one day. She forgot the glass was there and nearly knocked herself out slamming into it. When I made the mistake of laughing, she gave me the silent treatment for two days."

"Less than you deserved. George would have lectured you for a week straight."

"It worked, though. I never laughed at her again."

I was still doing door duty, though Henry was more eccentric than George or Nicky about using it. As June rolled to a close, he started asking to come in the back door instead of using George's window in the master bedroom. When I opened it, he'd say Prrrt!, turn his back and investigate the wood shed for a minute before coming in. I asked him several times why he did that and he always gave me a reply but, in spite of being a Cat Person, I couldn't understand a word.

"Maybe," said Ben, as we carried our drinks out to the pool, "he thinks making a mystery out of his entrance will keep you so interested that you won't commit lese felinity by refusing to open the door for him."

"Henry may be a smart cat," I said, "but I don't think his little head can hold such complicated concepts."

I sank into my deck chair and picked up my martini. Henry, lying on the concrete apron with one mischievous eye open, reached up and batted George gently on the rear as the king sauntered regally by.

"Look," I said, "Henry committed lese felinity!"

George ignored Henry's insolence, strolled a safe distance away and began bathing himself.

"George didn't hit back," I said. "Usually, he'd smack Henry across the face for that."

"Do you suppose the balance of power in our small kingdom has shifted slightly?"

"Between George and Henry perhaps. I doubt if our position has changed one iota."

And it hadn't, of course. The next morning George decided he'd prefer to drink his water exclusively from the bathtub. Soapy leftovers, which suited peasants like Henry, would not do. It had to be fresh water from the cold tap and I soon discovered that I was not allowed to put the plug in, but forced to come and turn the tap on for a fresh batch every time.

I told him there were two containers of water already available for his delectation and reminded him that the water was changed daily. He must have thought, if he paid attention at all, that I was complimenting him on his good taste because late that evening he again demanded a drink from the bathtub.

Ben said, as I came back to bed for the second time, "You're right; nothing has changed. We're still the slaves, no matter that Henry has shoved George half off his pedestal."

"I'd be willing to give Henry a little help," I muttered.

We began to notice that Henry didn't need any help. When he flopped down beside George on the veranda, the King merely opened one eye and went back to sleep again.

"Democracy at last," I said.

Ben laughed. "Democracy, hell! We used to have a feudal aristocracy. That's been softened to a benevolent dictatorship. Henry puts up with George being king – or dictator-for-life – but he doesn't put up with injustice. And George still punishes most instances of lese felinity."

I looked at Henry's cheerful face and ruffled fur. He still slept like a carelessly tossed banana skin.

"Gandhi in a torn t-shirt?"

"Don't waste time being fanciful," Ben said. "Remember your position and duties. George the Magnificent will want his dinner soon."

There was no need to mention Henry or Nicky. Unlike Gandhi, neither of them had ever missed a meal.

XVIII - EXHIBITIONS

In June Ben was back to using the pool almost every day. He loved playing in it but kept worrying about the pool cover motor breaking again and the disastrous effect on his budget. Every time he sat on the apron with the sun shining on him and a beer in his hand – his own personal definition of paradise – he began listing all the other things that could go wrong. He was doing such a good job of denigrating the pool that I didn't need to say a word.

"Sue was right when she called you eccentric," I said. "Why don't you just relax and enjoy it?" After all, if we were moving back to Victoria the following spring, he might as well make the most of the pool while he had the chance.

"Sue said we were both eccentric, not just me."

"It's fun being a bit odd. Look how much Cal Peterson enjoys life."

"He does some nice stuff, doesn't he?" Ben reached down to pat Nicky, who was lying beside the chair. "I wish we'd seen the wall hanging he won first prize for at the Saanichton fall fair last year."

"Me, too. I think it's great that living on a small island gives people a chance to do what they want without getting a lot of raised eyebrows. If I had the time and inclination, I'd start a delivery service. This island needs one and I've always wanted to drive a big truck."

"You have?" Ben eyed me as he took a swig of beer. "I never knew that."

"I'm full of little surprises. Aren't you?"

He stared at the glimmering pool for a moment. "Well, I'll admit I've got a yen to do something that's different. Every time I work with cement, I wonder if I could make sculptures with it."

"So why not try? Isn't that why we're here? To do all the things we couldn't do when we were working for other people?"

"I'd have to learn how."

"Well, I can't help you with that. Of course, if you want to take up knitting, I could teach you how to knit socks and sweaters."

Ben snorted. "I've better things to do with my time. Such as getting another beer."

When he came back, he said, "You know, I think George is depressed. He's been looking grumpy lately."

"I'll have Jerry give him a good going over. He needs to have his annual shots anyway."

"Good; I hate the idea of him being unhappy. Oh, and guess what Nicky was doing when I looked out the back door?"

"What?"

"Giving a mini exhibition of his prowess; herding baby chicks."

"And where was Mr. Mighty while this was going on?"

Ben laughed. "Ignoring the whole thing. I think he figures Nicky is his personal slave. Looks like everybody around here is a slave except George and Mr. Mighty."

"I wonder if the hen approves of Nicky herding her chicks." One of the Araucanas had nested under a blackberry hedge and was raising half a dozen babies. She was a busy little lady, bustling around the yard and clucking to the tiny yellow balls of fluff running along behind her, or sitting with her wings fluffed out, giving shelter to the chicks nestling beneath.

"I don't think she has much choice," Ben said. "Nicky is herding her, too."

A couple of days later we bundled George into the cat carrier. Henry took one look at the situation and, for the first time ever, went out the cat door, no doubt afraid we were thinking of caging him, too. Nicky paced and whined as if he was worried about his little tabby master being put into a box. The King, of course, was yelling loudly about the penalties for assaulting royalty.

Jerry's examination revealed that George had to have a tooth out and a cut in the roof of his mouth fixed. When we took him into the clinic the following week, he moaned to the staff that he'd been kidnapped and it was some other cat who should be having his tooth out. Nobody believed this tale and he was carried away to the operating room, big green eyes blinking at us over the attendant's shoulder.

We collected him at ten-thirty that evening and he yowled and tore ferociously at the cage all the way home.

"He must be terrified," Ben said. "He's never acted like this before."

"He's just furious at being treated in such a disrespectful way. Or else his mouth hurts and he's determined to get even with somebody or something."

It had been a harrowing day and I wanted to crawl into bed, but George had other ideas. Though Jerry had assured me the King would be groggy and probably sleep for days, His Magnificence purred and prowled and paced and yowled and demanded endless drinks in the bathtub. He finally settled down on my pillow at midnight and I fell asleep. An hour later he nagged me to get up and, no matter how deeply

I buried myself under the covers, I couldn't get away from those determined paws.

"I suppose you want out." I'd blocked all his usual exits because Jerry had recommended George use the litter box until late the next day. I got up, put on jeans and a sweatshirt and took him outside. He didn't seem groggy but Jerry had told me to watch him closely and I had visions of him staggering off over the horizon, lost, confused and unable to find his way home. He prowled like a miniature tiger, examining much of our five acres, but refused to use the flowerbeds, the vegetable garden or even the convenient pile of sand a road repair crew had left beside our gate.

He led me back to the house, apparently now as eager to go back to bed as I was. I showed him the litter box, in case he'd forgotten it was there, and went to bed. Ben began snoring. I poked him in the ribs. He continued to snore. Ten minutes later I gave up and moved to the couch. I'd barely fallen asleep when George complained in my ear. I burrowed deeper into my sleeping bag and ignored him.

He woke me again at three, his complaints turned up full volume, so I retreated to my studio and shut the door. After a while I drifted off but at four my own traitorous bladder woke me. I stumbled down the hall to the bathroom, went in without turning the light on and stepped squarely into the mess George had made on the small mat in front of the toilet.

When I'd got my foot and the mess cleaned up, I woke Ben. "That cat just showed his utter contempt for the way he was treated today."

"What?" Ben muttered fuzzily into his pillow.

"He made a statement on the bathroom mat. He says we are never to take him to the vet or the hospital again."

"You woke me up in the middle of the night to tell me that?"

"I am sick of that four-legged, fur-covered, mobile voice box yelling at me all night long. I am going to cut his tongue out, probably down around the kneecaps."

"You don't mean that."

"Yes, I do. George is just another version of the Chinese water torture. It's time somebody gave that cat his comeuppance."

Ben sat up in bed and stared at me. "But the poor little guy doesn't feel well."

"Just tell me this, St. Francis. Why does he keep me awake and let you sleep?"

"You're his mother." Ben turned his back and snuggled in his blankets.

What could I say? I knew George's mouth probably did hurt and that he was furious at us for letting it happen, but I couldn't do anything about that either. He was now sound asleep in Ben's chair. Four-thirty in the morning and all was quiet. Finally. I snuggled in my sleeping bag on the couch only to have Henry leap onto my chest and tell me a long complicated story about his own adventures.

Next day Ben put the freshly laundered bathroom mat back in place. "I wish there was a mobile vet service on the island. It would be much easier to have the vet come here when there's something wrong."

"I doubt it would make any difference."

"There'd be no more cat carriers," Ben said.

"George is still going to make statements about the treatment he gets. We were just lucky he chose the mat instead of the carpet."

"I guess."

"Anyway, Jerry says the reason he has no problem handling George and Henry is because they regard his office as his personal territory and, as guests, they instinctively behave themselves. George knuckles under to Jerry in his office the same way Clyde and Jeremy knuckled under to George when they were here. The mobile service would have to deal with them on their own turf."

"Okay, let's not worry about it. With any luck, we won't have to go through this again until Henry needs his shots." Ben pushed back his chair.

"Henry never makes statements. He takes things as they come and loves everybody. I'm sure if Henry had his way, every animal on the island would be invited in here for munchies and a game of tag. Have you noticed how he lets Nicky eat out of his dish?"

"Yeah, out of George's, too."

***

July was taken up with replacing the steps to the kitchen sliding doors with a cedar deck. Though I'd been campaigning for the deck since we'd moved in, Ben would have waited until he'd done a new budget if he hadn't tripped over a protruding nail in the rickety top step, fallen into a rose bush and achieved an intimate, painful acquaintance with several thorns.

The deck was ten by twenty feet with a low railing and two broad, sturdy steps down to the lawn. We put a small table and a couple of deck chairs out there so we could enjoy the late afternoon and evening sunlight when the front veranda, facing east, was in shadow. Soon the deck became a snoozing place for three lumps of fur; one small, dark and tiger-striped, one slightly larger and sprawled like a grey and white floor mop, and one big pure white lump which snored. They had discovered that the deck was the ultimate in convenience; they could hear a can-opener in the kitchen, see if anyone came down the drive and keep track of Ben in the garden all at the same time.

Next to the deck was a cedar shrub, twenty feet high and eight feet thick. Dozens of sparrows and house finches lived in it, supplied by the bird feeder Ben had hung under the eaves nearby. The branches were thick and almost impenetrable but too unstable for the cats to climb, though George gave plenty of thought to trying. The shrub seemed a safe place for birds until a Cooper's hawk swooped out of the sky and snatched a sparrow off a branch.

Ben and I were having breakfast and noticed nothing until the hawk mistook the sliding doors for open space and ricocheted off the glass. The sparrow escaped, losing only a few feathers. The hawk landed on the far side of the deck, upright but stunned, right between two sleeping cats.

George sat up on his haunches, eye to eye with the hawk, barely six inches from that lethal curved beak. Henry, two feet away, was struggling to his feet, a startled expression on his face.

Ben, noting the size and strength of the hawk's beak and claws, did his own pouncing. He ran across the deck and swept George up in his arms. The hawk, frightened into fast recovery, flew over the railing toward the meadow. Henry galloped after it while George sat and blinked. The action happened much faster than it takes to tell, and perhaps he thought he was dreaming. Henry, needless to say, didn't catch the hawk.

"He only chased it because he knew he couldn't catch it," I said.

Ben began picking up sparrow feathers. "George is a born hunter; Henry only does it for show."

"And because his mother told him he was supposed to."

After that, Henry sometimes pretended to hunt prey, to please George, but he galumphed along so clumsily on his big feet that the bird or mouse he was after was long gone by the time he was ready to pounce.

Soon the hunters became the hunted, the target of one of the most vicious and indomitable predators in the world. The fleas were back. In force.

When George and Henry began to scratch and chew themselves and a pinprick on my ankle proved to be a tiny black speck chewing on me, I knew I was in for weeks of torture and unbearable itching. I moaned to Ben and gazed out the window at the hot August day, praying for snow and a couple of weeks of below zero temperatures. "I don't understand why Nicky isn't getting bitten."

"There may be something about the chemical make-up of his skin that repels the fleas," Ben suggested.

"I'd say it was because they can't find their way through that thick fur."

Getting an ordinary comb through Nicky's fur was like trying to get a rake through a fifty-year-old growth of blackberry brambles. It was almost as bad using a flea comb on Henry's long fur. After I'd tugged for two or three minutes, he'd belt me with one of his big paws and do his disappearing act.

I hurried off to Mora Bay to see Jerry, hoping science had found an answer for fleas. He raved about some new stuff that could be given to the cats once a month. The idea was that the blood or moisture sucked from the cats would render the fleas' eggs infertile. Fleas would still bite the cats and me, but at least they wouldn't produce thousands more to leap at us from carpet and furniture.

"I'm tempted to try it," I told him, "but there'll be problems. George will throw up. I'll have to put Henry in the cat carrier and bring him to you for his injections or pills. Much as I hate fleas, I'm not sure this is going to work."

"No pills, no injections," he said. "It's a tasteless liquid you mix in with their food. They'll never even know it's there."

"Would it work on me?"

Jerry laughed, sure I was kidding. But I wasn't. The last time I'd researched fleas, I was horrified to learn that one flea can lay eight hundred eggs. An egg can remain dormant for months but, when conditions are right, it can develop into an adult flea in as little as eighteen days.

I said, "The human race may blow itself off the face of the earth, but fleas exhibit such a tenacity for life I'm sure they'll survive forever."

I bought a six-month supply of Jerry's wonderful new flea killer and came home. That evening, as I walked into the living room, a flea leapt off the carpet and bit me on the ankle.

"Ben," I said, "I know this is going to mess up your budget again, but Pied Piper is the only solution. We have to get rid of the fleas and eggs that are already in the house. Only then will this other stuff work."

"Okay. I know you're all suffering." He sighed. "We can take the animals and spend the day on the beach."

"I think I could bear that. We'll take a picnic lunch for everybody. And by the way, I've thought of a possible name for the farm. Flea Circus."

He didn't bother even commenting on that one.

When I went to the kitchen at ten to make a pot of tea, a masked face – a small furry one – was peering through the sliding door.

"Ben, there's a raccoon on the deck."

He dashed in from the living room. "This is the first time I've seen one close up. Maybe they hide under the deck for safety. Nicky's too big to crawl under there."

I wanted to say that Nicky was such a wimp he'd run from any animal that didn't purr at him, but Ben was getting sensitive to my comments about his guard dog.

"I wonder if putting dog kibbles out for them would keep them away from the garbage can," he said. "They're probably hungry."

"You didn't tell me they'd been at the garbage can."

"It's only happened the last three nights. I found out they can get the lid off even when it's weighted down with bricks."

"I don't think you should encourage them. They might start killing the chickens."

"If I feed them all the time, they won't need to bother the chickens. Or the garbage cans."

"What if they go after George or Henry? They're much stronger than a cat and just as fast."

"Ginna's right, you worry too much," Ben said. "George and Henry are exceptionally bright cats. They know better than to bother a raccoon. Besides, I'd like to watch the raccoons and see what they do."

Ben put a dish of kibble on the deck for the raccoons. We sat quietly at the kitchen table and after a few moments, three young ones joined their mother on the deck. When the kibble was gone, all four sat in a row at the glass door and stared in at us.

"They look like a band about to sing for their supper."

"They're cute little guys," said St. Francis. "I'll give them more food. I'd better put some water out, too."

"Fine. Just don't ask me to treat them for fleas."

XIX - THE ROYAL INFIRMARY

Ben's ploy of feeding the raccoons worked well; we had no further trouble with garbage cans. But he finally had to admit that Nicky would never learn to chase deer. After we harvested the last of the vegetables, delivered them to the supermarket in Mora Bay, and put the pool to bed, Ben decided to build a deer-proof fence around the garden.

I thought this was a waste of time. Our two years on the farm would be over in early spring and if we weren't here to plant a garden, why bother with a fence? But I kept my thoughts to myself and repeated my well-used mantra: whatever we spent on the farm would add to its value.

Building the new fence involved ripping out the old one, deepening the post holes and cementing in taller posts, then stringing wire to a height of eight feet. Nicky, intrigued by our activity, seemed to think he should fill the holes for us. Sometimes we had to dig out a hole two or three times before we got the post in.

When the job was done, Ben hefted two leftover bags of cement into the wheelbarrow. Henry, who'd been lying in the grass, supervising, hopped up and sat on them.

Ben knelt and petted him. "What do you think, Henry? Should I give sculpture a try? Do I have time?"

Henry rubbed his nose against Ben's.

"Okay, I will." Ben looked at me. "Henry's suited to island life, isn't he? Not only does he refuse to hunt, he's artistic, too. Very eccentric cat."

October was lovely, the earth at that quiescent stage between full ripeness and the beginning of decay. We all slowed to match its pace and wandered around the farm and down to the beach or lazed in mellow sunshine. Even rejection slips from magazine editors didn't lessen my joy in golden maple leaves and cobalt skies. I merely printed off new copies of my stories and mailed them to other magazines. The days passed like amber beads on a string and I savoured each one, knowing that next fall I'd be enjoying fall colours and cobalt skies in Victoria.

One evening toward the end of the month, Ben and I prepared for the next morning's jaunt to the animal clinic with George. His Imperial Fussiness had to have his teeth cleaned and, judging by what this had cost the year before, the procedure probably included gold fillings, not to mention having his gums rebuilt, his whiskers waxed and the hair in his ears curled.

George was not allowed to have food or drink after midnight, so Ben went around dumping water dishes, wiping up the moisture in the bathtub, hiding cat food and locking doors.

I fell asleep at eleven, exhausted from just thinking about putting George in the cat carrier, but was wakened at two-thirty by Henry. "What do you want, you miserable bundle of fur?"

After much thought and three minutes of licking his left hind leg, he decided he wanted to go out. George wanted to go out, too, but I couldn't allow that in case he drank water from puddles in the orchard. I locked George in Ben's den and opened the back door for Henry.

Five minutes later Henry sat at the deck door, pawing the glass and looking pitiful. I invited him to enter. He gave his right hind leg a good wash and finally did me the favour of strolling in. Assuming that Henry might want to go out again, I left George in the den. The less I had to do when roused from a deep sleep the better.

I went to the kitchen to get a glass of milk and discovered Ben had dumped the water out of a burnt pan that was meant to be soaking, but had left both cat food dishes, full of water, in the sink. Since he knew George could easily jump onto the kitchen counter and might drink the forbidden water, I was puzzled. But, at that hour, I was rarely able to do more than put one foot in front of the other so I dumped the water out and gave up trying to understand his logic.

When I was back in bed, Henry immediately jumped on my chest, settled down, and rumbled like a motor boat. Within seconds Ben began to snore.

I don't mind other people snoring – provided I can't hear it – but in spite of a dozen pokes with my elbow, Ben went on being noisy. I collected my sleeping bag and pillow and bedded down on the couch. I was immediately joined by Henry, who thumped heavily onto my chest again, kneading and purring. By now I was wide awake. After what seemed like hours, I started to plot a new short story and fell asleep at once.

At three minutes after four, Ben wandered into the living room, waking me up.

"Why is George locked in my den?" he asked.

I could have said a great deal about logic, and about people who snore and also ask dumb questions at four in the morning, but I restrained myself.

"I can't let one cat out and in and keep the other cat in unless I hang onto him with both hands which means I don't have any hands left to open doors."

"Huh?"

I rolled over and feigned sleep.

The Houseboy felt sorry for George and let him out of the den before he went back to bed. His Magnificence immediately joined Henry and me, plumping down on my thighs and hanging on with his claws. At least he didn't purr. About five, I noticed snow flakes drifting down. After a wistful moment of regret for the end of autumn, I tried to decide whether the snow was Good because it would freeze fleas to death or Bad because it might interfere with driving. Then I drifted off.

At five-thirty Henry signified his desire to go out again by sticking his claws in one of the stereo speakers. Startled, I leapt off the couch, dislodging George. I locked the King in my studio and Henry outside and crawled, muttering, back into the sleeping bag.

When George was shut in the studio, he was too far away for his loud complaining to keep me awake. But ten minutes later, Henry jumped from the veranda to the window sill three feet from my head, clawed at the glass and yowled.

I let Henry in. He said he wanted food. I gave him food. He decided he didn't want it.

I knew why. His mouth was infected again, although it had been only a month since his teeth were cleaned and two of them pulled. The night before, he'd tried to eat some soft food, the human equivalent of a lettuce leaf, and cried with pain. He was extremely hungry by this time and kept asking why I insisted on dishing out food that bit him. He wasn't impressed by the news that veterinarians aren't up and about in the middle of the night.

Strangely enough, it was soon six a.m. I knew that if I managed to fall sleep again, I'd never hear the alarm and would therefore miss George's seven-thirty appointment at the clinic. So I got up, brushed my teeth and washed some dishes while George cried in the studio. I felt so guilty about shutting him in that it came out as anger and I yelled down the hall, "Be quiet, you spoiled streak of stripes – if you think life is tough now, wait an hour!" I'm sure it didn't make him feel any better and it only made me feel worse.

At twenty to seven, I tiptoed loudly into the bedroom, waking up Ben. At ten after seven, he sneaked the cat carrier into the hall, causing Henry to panic. Since all the doors were shut, he was reduced to trying to claw his way through the thermal pane glass to the deck. George, snarling at this latest infringement of his dignity, was popped into the cage and we departed into the chilly dawn.

"It's really cold this morning," Ben complained.

"There was snow during the night."

"You must have dreamt it. We never get snow this early."

I held my tongue.

At the clinic, we signed George in, removed his red collar and handed him to a young attendant. When she told him he was incredibly gorgeous, he kicked her and tried to dive back into the cat carrier. Her soothing manner masked a businesslike grip, however, and George was carted off. It was the Houseboy's turn to feel guilty.

"The poor old King! He's going to be locked in one of those hospital cages until after lunch. I wish Jerry could have scheduled the surgery for this morning."

Back home, I waited until nine, when Jerry's office opened, then phoned to make an appointment for Henry. The receptionist said, "We have a cancellation. Can you get here in 20 minutes?" It took desperate determination to get Henry, howling in protest and wielding all eight legs and 200 claws, into the cat carrier.

"Henry," I pleaded, "we aren't being mean to you. I'm sorry to do this, but the vet has to look at your mouth and get rid of the pain. We think you're wonderful and adorable and all the rest of it."

Ben grunted.

Henry wailed.

When we got to the vet's office, Jerry examined Henry and said, "He's only got one tiny little red patch on his gum." He gave the cat a shot of antibiotic and us a lecture on the multiple dangers of letting cats go outside, and recommended a blood test.

I carried Henry to the cat cage and he leapt in all by himself, hunched down and looked at me imploringly.

"Can we get the test done now?" I asked. "I don't think we'll be able to get him back in the carrier again if we go home and let him out."

By ten we were at the clinic and Henry was carried away to the lab. Ben wanted to go in the back and visit George, who was in a cage, waiting for his operation, and no doubt fuming and dreaming up punishments for us.

"Don't do that," I said. "He'll think you've come to take him home and he'll be even unhappier when you walk away and leave him there."

Fifteen minutes later, when the attendant brought Henry back from the lab and put him in the carrier, I approached the desk to pay for the lab tests, which the last time had cost $30.

With a sweet smile, the receptionist said, "That will be $140.00, please." Ben moaned. The lab technician came out and explained in ten-syllable words the procedures she'd carried out. Ben looked in his wallet, shook his head and reached for his checkbook.

Three miles from home, we saw Nicky trotting along the road, wearing his usual Samoyed grin.

"I thought you shut him in the house," Ben said.

"Well, I meant to, but I must have forgotten."

Ben stopped the car and I got out and opened the back door. "Nicky, you're a bad boy. Get in here this minute." He obligingly hopped onto the back seat beside the cat carrier and sat on his blanket, looking pleased with himself. I reached back and patted him. Henry squirmed restlessly in the carrier and hissed.

When we pulled into the driveway, there was Nicky sitting on the back steps. As soon as the car stopped, he came running to meet us.

Ben stared at the Nicky in the back seat. "If that's our Nicky in the yard, then who is this?"

"I don't know. But I guess we'd better take him back where we found him." Our own Nicky had already demonstrated the Samoyed wandering tendency.

"I'll do it," Ben said. "You take Henry and our Nicky inside."

Henry was delighted to be home again. He demanded food. He refused food. My load of guilt was growing by the minute. Ben came back and made coffee and I inhaled two cups nonstop.

At three-thirty, Jerry phoned to say George had had a tooth out and, though he was high on pain-killer, he'd be ready to come home by six. At one minute after the hour we arrived at the clinic to collect him, this time having made sure Nicky was locked in the house.

While George was held for ransom somewhere in the labyrinth of mysterious corridors, the receptionist presented a bill for $311.27. Ben, looking grim, handed over his VISA card. An attendant brought George out and popped him in the carrier.

On the way home, I comforted Ben. "Think of all the advantages we have. We're tired and the budget is blown but we have a bed to sleep in and three cuddly, furry companions to reduce our level of stress and improve our health."

During the next minute or two, I discovered that Ben hadn't forgotten one word of what he learned in the armed services about swearing.

George was definitely high. He fell off furniture and staggered into things. The anaesthetic had enlarged his pupils and he couldn't see in bright light. He snarled when approached and yelled when touched. He seemed unsure of who he was, where he was or what he meant to do next.

Henry was still woozy on antibiotic and his right hind leg kept collapsing at the most inopportune times, such as when he tried to get up on a kitchen chair. He put his front paws on the chair cushion and tried to heave his rear end up, but his hind leg gave way and he slid all the way under the chair on his back, still clinging to the cushion with his front paws. He retracted the claws, fell to the floor, got up and staggered drunkenly away.

At ten p.m. Ben's brother, David, phoned from Moose Jaw to say that he'd found a nursing home with a vacancy and that their mother could move in the following week if only he could talk her into it. There was much discussion about Edith's intense repugnance for such places and her refusal to admit she needed care. Giddy with exhaustion, I stopped just short of suggesting that with all the experience Ben and I had gained in just one day with the cats, we could take the cat carrier to Moose Jaw and it would all be over in five minutes.

***

Veterinarians are very caring and sometimes perform miracles, but their service lacks one important item. They do not come to your home and dose the resident royals with the prescribed medicine. Jerry left this task to me with an airy wave of his hand, saying, "It's simple. Just wrap the cat in a towel and pop the pill down his throat."

I had once had occasion to wrap a cat in a towel in order to shove medicine down his throat and all I achieved was one mad cat, one shredded towel and the medicine all over me instead of inside the cat. And, for the next six months, every time the cat saw me with a towel in my hand, he disappeared for hours.

After reading the instructions for the medicine, I grumbled to Ben, "I'll have to get up half an hour earlier every day to con those two into swallowing their pills."

"Jerry said all you have to do is wrap the cat ..."

Snarling, I retreated to my studio. That night I took the instructions to bed to memorize because I had a pretty fair idea what life would be like in the morning.

As usual, the two steps prior to climbing out of bed were easy: waking up and getting my eyes open. George and Henry helped by meowing, nudging, and patting my face with their dear little paws. Putting on a dressing gown and finding my glasses I was able to manage all by myself.

In the kitchen, I washed out two cat dishes and opened a can of the strongest-tasting cat food available. By this time, the royals were 'catting' my heels and wanting to know what was taking me so long.

Then I had to organize the medicine.

George's, half a pink pill every day, required good hand-eye coordination and patience. I had to put the pill on a flat surface and split it in half with a razor blade. A simple operation, except that both cats were yelling at me to hurry up and my aim was off, resulting in a pill cut into one-third and two-thirds and spattered with blood from the slash in my finger. After that, I merely had to grind the pill with a small mortar and pestle and mix it into his food.

Henry had to have two medicines each day. One was a small white tablet, ground to dust and mixed with his food. No problem. The other was one fourth of a capsule of antibiotic. The antibiotic was a yellow powder contained in a capsule which supposedly melted away in the stomach.

This had to be pure fantasy on the part of the pill merchants. The only thing that would slice into it was an exceedingly sharp razor blade and even then it just bent itself out of shape until I got downright vicious, which resulted in a spray of yellow powder all over me and the kitchen counter.

Once the capsule was open, the powder had to be divided into four equal portions. No difficulty here – but where could I keep three tiny piles of yellow powder so they'd be easy to deal with in the mental fog of morning? After searching the house, the only suitable containers I could find were china egg cups.

By this time, the royals were ordering me to produce their breakfast and threatening to sell me back to the slave dealer if it didn't appear at once.

But I had still more medicine to deal with. Henry was supposed to have one millilitre of Vitamin B complex every 12 hours in order to give him more zest for life. I checked my metric conversion table. Fifteen millilitres equalled one-half ounce, or one tablespoon. Therefore one teaspoon would be seven and a half millilitres. Sounded like an eighth teaspoon was about right. One more lesson I'd been forced to learn: a millilitre was about two drops.

I wasn't convinced that Henry, who loved to play, needed Vitamin B. He chased the King all over the house in his eagerness to wrestle. It was only George's ability to leap on top of the piano that saved his tail and dignity from Henry's playful mauling. Every day Henry climbed forty feet up the Garry oak tree beyond the orchard and talked to the squirrels. I'd heard that he also visited our neighbours on either side and across the road and played with the resident animals. If Henry acquired more zest for life, nobody would have any peace.

However, Jerry had assured me that the stuff smelled like liver and cats adored it, so I mixed a couple of drops in Henry's food and gave George some as a treat. The cats took one sniff and tried to bury the food. I had to dump it out, wash the dishes, spoon out more food and grind up more pills. So much for the universal popularity of Vitamin B complex.

And so the days went. If I was lucky, the royals ate their food and medicine. Some mornings I wasn't lucky, which meant opening a different kind of cat food and starting all over again.

On the fifth morning, I said to Ben, "It would be a lot simpler to take the cats to the vet and let him dose them. All we'd have to do is put the cats in carriers and drive them into Mora Bay. Oh yes, and talk Jerry into opening his office at seven a.m. seven days a week."

"Holly, you're cracking up. Maybe you should see the doctor."

"He'd just prescribe pills and tell you to wrap me in a towel before you shoved them down my throat."

XX - THE IMPERIAL BEDCHAMBER

Winter came, cold and bleak, in November. The wind blew in off the sea, rain poured down day after day, and the lab report on Henry came back saying that he had Feline Immunodeficiency Virus. Jerry told us that FIV was fatal and, like HIV in humans, there was no cure. Henry might live six months or six years; there was no way of telling.

"Those gum infections are a result of the FIV," Jerry said. "My guess is that he got it when he was a street cat and was attacked by an infected cat."

"What about George? Could he get it from Henry?"

"Only if George's mouth comes in direct contact with Henry's blood or saliva. For example, if George bit Henry and got Henry's blood in his mouth, or if Henry bit George and his saliva got into George's veins. They don't fight, do they?"

I was close to tears. So was Ben. "Henry's a Buddhist. He doesn't believe in violence."

"Well, I wouldn't worry then. And you never know; Henry could live for years. Just take good care of him."

Henry's gum infection cleared up quickly and he was back to his usual frisky self, climbing trees, batting at Nicky's tail, pestering George. I began to lean toward Buddhism myself. Henry was happy living one day at a time, one moment at a time, and he didn't worry. I thought how much better life would be if I could live that way, too. I sent off another short story and two poems I'd written about George and Henry. Why worry about rejections? Why worry about Henry, when I was doing all I could for him? But the latter was far easier said than done.

The days grew shorter and George and Henry became professional nap artists, especially on dark rainy days. Even Nicky, fed up with rain and Ben's boring occupations of stripping wallpaper in one of the upstairs bedrooms or sitting in his den poring over greenhouse plans, spent hours curled up in his blanket-covered chair.

The cats' first choice was a warm lap, but the owner of the lap had to sit still — no sneezing, coughing or other disturbing noises — nor did they approve of the lap disappearing to answer the telephone or calls of nature. They competed for the same lap, even when a second was available, and it took dedication to read a book and drink coffee with two cats jockeying for position.

It took dedication to have a nap myself. When I lay on my side, Henry balanced himself on my ribs and shoulder so he could tickle my face with his long whiskers and snore in my ear. George perched on my hip. If I moved even a little, they dug their claws in for balance.

The only way I could avoid having nap mates was to take my clothes off; neither cat liked lying on bare skin. But that was hardly a practical solution when I might be required to answer the door at any time in my role of Egg Lady. I wondered if the cats thought something was wrong when I wasn't wearing 'fur.' I suspect the answer was much simpler; bare skin didn't provide good purchase for their claws.

George had a broad choice of sleeping places by virtue of his ability to float from crag to crag on the Alps of our furniture. Clumsy Henry could jump only three feet; after that he clawed his way up paw over paw.

One day, however, Henry discovered he could jump from our bedroom armchair to Ben's chest of drawers. This was where Ben tossed loose change, keys, bits of paper, stray buttons and anything else he didn't know where to file. Henry's leaps scrunched the dresser scarf into ridges and knocked piles of stuff onto the floor. He'd curl up in the middle of the remaining debris and, when dreaming, kick more things overboard.

When George discovered his subordinate had beaten him to this 'in' place, he insinuated himself into Henry's place, forcing Henry to retreat to the low dresser next to the chest of drawers.

The Houseboy, noting Henry's forlorn expression, said, "Poor little guy. I'll give him a folded towel to lie on."

Henry curled up on the towel. An hour later, George had booted Henry off and was occupying its exact centre.

Ben put another towel on the dresser. George promptly claimed that but Henry took over the original one. George paced, trying to figure out how to sleep on both towels at once. Failing, he declared a truce.

The dresser was 'in' for about six weeks. Every morning we straightened the scarves, picked debris off the floor and smoothed the towels. The royals slept peacefully.

When I dared to complain, St. Francis said, "They're people, too. They're entitled to sleep where they want."

Suddenly, the dresser was 'out.' Henry learned to gain Ben's desk by hopping up on his easy chair, then wriggling behind the drapes along the windowsill to step down onto the desk. He didn't seem to mind sleeping on a hard desk, even with George nudging him towards the edge.

Ben put a fat feather pillow on the desk next to the window. Both cats slept there, basking in the sun, if there was any, and occasionally raising their heads to watch birds and squirrels playing in the trees outside. The pillow was big enough for two cats and we hoped the rivalry would end.

Not so. The half of the pillow nearest the window became the prized spot. One afternoon George settled smugly into it while Henry stared at him. After a few moments, Henry stepped over George, sat on the edge of the desk and gazed out the window. His big, fluffy tail swept back and forth across George's face. The King put up with this for perhaps thirty seconds before he jumped down in disgust. Henry settled into the sunny end of the pillow with a smile on his face and a rumbling purr.

Next they competed for the top of my printer, which had room for only one cat, so the other slept beside it, awaiting his opportunity. When Henry moved to my keyboard, I complained about cat hair getting into my equipment.

"They're guarding your computer so nobody will steal it," Ben said. "You should be grateful to those cats for their loyalty and devotion."

I said something rude. Ben went to his workshop and made sturdy plywood covers for both printer and keyboard. I topped the covers with towels, but the royals lost interest and moved to my desk.

Although grateful to have the use of my keyboard again, I was still unhappy about cat hair drifting around. I also didn't like the strange sentences the cats wrote on the screen as they walked across the keyboard on their way out of the room. Neither of them could spell.

Bored with my studio, the cats moved to an armchair in the living room, where Henry became as adept at kicking George off as George was at kicking Henry off. That finally palled and the chair was occupied most of the day by two mounds of fur. Occasionally one would wake up, glare at the other, decide it was too much trouble to argue, and go back to sleep again.

On the coldest days, the cats slept on Nicky. Henry would snuggle between Nicky's paws and George would lie on the dog's back. Nicky seemed happy to share his chair with the royals – until one of them tried to knead him. Then he shook them off and climbed up on our bed to sleep.

When George wearied of sharing his bed with social inferiors, he did his Superman act. A favourite spot was under a small lamp on top of the television cabinet. He knew the Houseboy would turn on the lamp so he could bask in its heat. When he awoke and sat up, his head trapped under the small lamp shade, he looked as though he'd just come home from a wild party. Another favourite was the walk-in linen closet and he'd look up at the door knob and yell for someone to open the door. He perched on the towel shelf at eye level – mine, not his – and every time he leapt up, kicked piles of towels on the floor, which his slaves then had to replace.

The linen closet wasn't my favourite, however. I'd forget he was in there, wander in for a towel and jump when I saw malevolent green eyes glaring at me out of the dark. Ben, always tidy, would routinely shut the door on his way by without checking to see if George was occupying a shelf. Hours later we'd hear a faint yowling and, the first few times, opened front and back doors and even went outside to look for him before we realised he was in the closet.

When George escaped to high places, Henry often slept in a paper grocery bag, under a couch or among the shoes in a closet. When we wanted to be sure Henry was in the house, we had to crawl around on our hands and knees looking for him. It was astonishing what small, inaccessible places that cat could get into and even more astonishing how many such places there were in our house.

Ben's favourite armchair was also George's. As soon as Ben left it, George dove into the chair and feigned sleep. When Ben returned and picked him up, the King squeaked pathetically. If Ben remained hardhearted and sat in the chair, George sat on Ben. Both grumbled, but neither would move. At such times it was left to me to attend to the phone, the door, the television and mashing the potatoes for our supper. If Henry was sitting in my lap, nothing got done.

***

Ben now felt sorry for the deer because they couldn't get into the vegetable garden and began feeding them as well as the raccoons. Nicky was happy to be working again, herding the deer in a tight group while they munched. When they finished, he frantically tried to round them up as they wandered away. It usually took them an hour or so to shake him off and disappear into the trees. Nicky would come home, tongue lolling out, and sit at Ben's feet, waiting for praise.

"How many more animals are you going to adopt?" I asked.

"I haven't adopted them. It's just that they're hungry and there's nothing for them to eat right now."

The deer had survived before Ben came along and I was sure they'd go on surviving without him, but I handed over all the vegetable scraps and bought huge sacks of carrots at the feed store whenever I drove into Mora Bay. Ben gave me frequent updates on what the deer liked and didn't like.

"They won't eat onion," he said. "Bread is okay if there's nothing else but they really love pumpkin. Next year I'll have to plant more than a couple of rows. If I could get a greenhouse going, I'd have lettuce and celery for them all year long."

"Keep enough for us," I said, not wanting to remind him that we wouldn't be on the farm next year. I carried the salad bowl to the dining room table, only to discover that George and Henry were lying in the middle of it again.

This was the most recent 'in' place and I felt George had gone too far. One afternoon I'd removed him from the table nine times in fifteen minutes, my admonitions progressing from a gentle, "Sweetie, this table is not for cats," to a screaming, red-faced, "Get off there, you miserable flea-bitten wretch; I said NO!"

But George could out-stubborn me without even trying. Defeated, we now removed place mats and spread sleeping towels on the table for the cats as soon as dinner was over.

"If I had as much determination as that cat, I could rule the world," I said to Ben, as I put the salad on the sideboard.

Both cats squawked as I lifted them off the table. They hovered as we removed the towels, wiped off cat hair, laid the table and put our food down. They hovered as we ate, only slightly distracted by little treats of chicken off our plates. The minute we took the empty plates out to the kitchen, they reclaimed the territory. This battle for supremacy had made the dining room table an 'in' place far longer than usual.

That evening I was hosting the weekly bridge game. I ignored the outraged complaints as I removed the royals again, laid a new cloth and put out the cards, score pads, ashtrays and pencils. Onto the sideboard went a plate of cookies, napkins, and glasses ready for drinks. George and Henry, sensing I meant business, sought temporary roosts.

The game proceeded without incident for a couple of hours. Then Henry decided I'd been allowed to have my own way long enough. While I was in the kitchen getting fresh drinks, he jumped from my chair onto the table. I returned just as he stretched out on the dummy hand.

"Kindly remove that cat or I'll trump him," Frank said, favouring Henry with a benevolent smile.

I removed Henry and rearranged the cards. He tried twice again to sabotage the game before Jerry lifted Henry onto his knees. "He can sleep on my lap for awhile." Jerry rubbed Henry's head.

George made one minor attempt to reclaim the table by leaping up onto the three inches of space between the plate of cookies and the edge of the sideboard. He teetered precariously and I didn't know whether to rescue him or the cookies. I chose the cookies, figuring that if George fell off backwards, he could roll over in mid-air and land on his feet. The cookies were helpless.

It wasn't until Jerry, Cindy and Frank left, much later than George thought they should have, that he tried again. As I was putting beer mugs on the kitchen counter, I heard a loud crash. I rushed into the dining room to find that George had leapt onto the table and skidded across it, sliding the cloth half off. Scattered on the carpet were two decks of cards, five pencils, four score pads, two empty glasses, three expiring ice cubes and, upside down, a dish of peanuts and the ashtray.

George studied the mess with considerable interest, then looked at me. Now how did that happen?

I removed him, straightened the cloth and laid out his towel. I picked up the debris. I refrained from screaming only because Ben was asleep.

George chose the next 'in' place by clawing a bath towel off the bar onto the heat register below and curling up on it. Henry bedded down on the toilet seat, which was covered with thick, soft material. Soon George joined him. It was a fine location for them, but inconvenient for us.

When I stumbled half asleep to the bathroom in the dark, it was disconcerting to find I couldn't lift the toilet seat. By the time I realized it was weighed down by 25 pounds of cat, they were awake and protesting. I dumped them on the floor and they retaliated by scrambling back up onto my warm bare knees. We considered tramping upstairs to use the other bathroom.

"It hardly seems worth the trouble," I said. "George is determined to sleep on whatever we want to use."

"He just likes to be close to us," St. Francis replied.

Soon the bathroom was 'out.' I was not comforted. The cats regularly recycled their sleeping places and a few weeks later the bathroom would be 'in' again, just as the bedroom dresser was now regaining its popularity.

Henry started it. He leapt onto my dresser, skidded on the dresser scarf, smacked into the wall and ricocheted onto my jewellery case.

Since he hadn't quite knocked it off the dresser, he sat on it, excess parts of him sagging over the edges. It was too small to sleep on so he left, scrambling the dresser scarf into a complete mess and knocking my antique doll to the floor. Having achieved an appropriately lived-in look for the bedroom, he curled up on the bed and went happily to sleep.

Later I found George asleep in the laundry sink.

"Good thing there wasn't a wash going through," I told him. "You'd have been soaked when the washer drained."

Perhaps he did occasionally listen to what I said, because next day he was curled up in the newspaper recycling box. I put a towel on top of the papers and he was happy there for some time.

"It's as good a spot as any," Ben said. "If he gets recycled along with the newspapers, at least he's got eight more lives to go."

XXI - WINTER GAMES

The first snowfall came a week before Christmas. It wasn't the usual wet, heavy, slippery snow that snarls traffic and frays tempers, but a light dusting that kept us nervously watching out the window for the real thing. Nicky thought it was wonderful stuff to play with. He raced around, barking at the flakes falling on his nose, and pawed at the inch or so that had accumulated on the ground.

George, however, regarded snow as a cold, wet insult to Royal feet and shook each paw after picking it up. His progress across the back yard was slow, his expression grumpy. Henry, well padded with thick fur, flopped down and looked at the other two as though they were crazy.

"Did I ever tell you about my Aunt Ruth's cat, Sheba?" I asked Ben when he rose to pour a second breakfast coffee.

He looked resigned. "All right, it's a snowy morning and I have nothing better to do. Go ahead."

"I spent a couple of weeks over Christmas with Ruth one year and every day I took Sheba outside to play. She liked to tunnel in deep snow and pop up every few feet. She probably thought she was surprising me, but I could see the snow collapsing behind her as she burrowed."

Ben poured the coffee. "I wouldn't have thought Siamese liked snow. Then what happened?"

"Nothing."

"That wasn't a story. That wasn't even an anecdote." Ben removed Henry from the editorial page for the third time that morning.

"I have a real Sheba story."

Henry walked in front of Ben, affectionately brushing the Houseboy's chin with his big frothy tail, and flopped on the newspaper again. Ben cuddled him. "Poor old Henry. You can lie on the editorial if you want." He looked at me. "So tell me the story."

Aunt Ruth used to let Sheba out in the morning and watch her from the kitchen window. When Sheba finished tormenting the dog, she'd climb onto the tool shed roof. Soon half a dozen cats would join her. After planning the day's hunt and gossiping about the difficulty of getting good slaves, they'd disappear. Ruth didn't know where they went or what they did until a neighbour spoke to her later.

"Is this the first cat you've owned?" she asked, pointing at the lean and elegant Sheba.

"About the twentieth, I believe," Aunt Ruth said, puzzled. "Why do you ask?"

"Oh, just wondering."

A few days later, another neighbour stopped my aunt in the street. "That dear little cat of yours is very thin," she said. "Had you noticed?"

It turned out that Sheba visited several houses on the street every day, begging for food in a weak little voice and gulping whatever she was given. The neighbours were sure Aunt Ruth had been starving her.

Ben put down his coffee mug. "Siamese cats always look like they're starving." Since being enslaved by George, he'd read every cat book in the Mora Bay library and was now ordering them from other libraries.

That night we were wakened by a distinctly feline wailing outside. In dressing gowns and slippers, we opened every door and looked out. The pitiful meowing continued, but no matter how hard we peered into the drifting snow flakes, we couldn't see a cat anywhere.

"Let's find out if George and Henry are in the house," said Ben. "It could be one of the neighbours' cats."

We looked into, under, on top of, behind and beside everything in the house. Henry snored on the couch and Nicky slept in his chair, but there was no George. We went into the snowstorm and stood on the kitchen deck, calling.

"Meow!" came the forlorn cry. But where was he?

"Meow!" I could have sworn that one had come from above and behind me.

It had. George was on the roof.

I stretched my arms up toward the eaves. "Come on, George. I can catch you."

He teetered on the edge, meowing, but refused to jump.

I bent over. "Jump on my back, George." I'd have claw marks for weeks, but I was willing to pay any price to get back to my warm bed.

George had no intention of trusting his precious body to an unreliable slave. He moaned some more and disappeared over the top of the roof. We brushed snow off ourselves and ran through the house and out the front door, calling.

He decided he couldn't climb down the veranda roof, either, and continued his heartrending cries.

"His feet must be freezing," Ben said. "I wonder how long he's been stranded up there."

I remembered there were two gnarled oak trees beside the house on the north side. It seemed obvious that he'd climbed onto the roof from one of those and Ben agreed.

"Well, if he went up that way, he can come down that way," I said, suddenly suspecting that George was teasing us. "I'm going back inside."

The Houseboy was shocked. "We can't just leave him! He's probably forgotten how he got up there. He might slip and fall, with all this snow."

I couldn't convince Ben that George would come down on his own if we quit playing his silly game. He got the rickety old step-ladder from the workshop and set it up on the cedar deck.

"You go up," he said. "You're lighter than me."

I climbed as high as I dared, nervous of damaging my own precious body. George came to the eaves and nuzzled my hand. I grabbed him and tried to swing him up and out, away from the roof, so I could hand him to Ben, but George got a death grip on the metal lip of the eaves and refused to let go. The ladder quaked under my freezing cold feet.

"George, cooperate! I'm rescuing you from death by exposure."

Desperation and brute strength finally did the trick. I handed George to Ben and crawled down the ladder.

Inside the house, George let out a triumphant yowl, which woke Nicky and Henry, and raced up and down the hall a few times. His shivering servants made themselves cocoa and took their frozen feet back to bed.

A couple of days later, when the snow had melted, I happened to look out the bathroom window just as George skittered up the oak tree outside. He balanced himself in the Y of two tiny branches and leapt across three feet of empty space to the roof.

After a moment he began meowing. Piteously.

I poured a cup of coffee and leaned on the bathroom window sill, prepared to wait and watch for as long as it took George to decide to come down again.

Sure enough, he got tired of crying wolf and came to the edge of the roof. He floated effortlessly through the air to the Y of the branch, walked daintily down a larger branch to the main trunk, then saw me. He raced down the tree head first, around the corner of the house and in through the cat door, doing a gloating Siamese yell.

Needless to say, he never again asked to be rescued from the roof. Cats know that a practical joke is only funny if the victims don't catch on.

Ben and I noticed, as we were hanging ornaments on the Christmas tree, that George's sense of humour extended only to his own jokes. He was not amused when Henry, lying in wait behind a door, pounced on him when he walked by. The King squawked, wriggled out from under Henry's big paws and leapt to safety on the bookcase. Henry tried to coax him down with bird-like trills but the King refused to damage his dignity by joining in Henry's frivolity.

"Come to think of it," Ben said, "it's hard to imagine George as a baby. He's so dignified and self-important now that he must have been one solemn little kitten."

"He's a lot more playful than when we first got him."

"Only when it's his idea." George would sometimes condescend to bat the crumpled tea bag envelopes he'd trained us to throw for him, but he did it with an air of doing us a big favour. "But you're right. I guess he's finally sure he owns us and the farm."

"He wouldn't have let Henry stay otherwise."

George also liked chasing string when he was in the mood, but if Henry joined the act there was chaos. They each demanded exclusive possession and ended up chasing each other instead. I tried dragging two pieces of string around but they zeroed in on the same one or stalked off, unable to deal with the stress of deciding which string was the Royal one. They sometimes stared at me as though puzzled that I would pretend one string was as good as another.

Ben finished arranging the Christmas lights and I draped the last handful of icicles on the branches. We stood back to admire our handiwork.

"This calls for a drink," Ben said. "We may as well start the celebrating early."

"Crush some catnip for His Magnificence, too."

Ben laughed. "Good idea. He hasn't been drunk and disorderly since he ate it in the garden last summer."

Catnip was the only thing that got George off his high horse. After three nibbles, his eyes crossed and his muscles lost coordination. Four nibbles and he'd roll over on his back, expression blissful, legs flopping in every direction. Sobriety brought, not remorse, but an exaggerated hauteur which denied the episode had ever happened. Life for Henry was already enough fun; he never bothered with catnip.

Ben brought our drinks and we sat down to admire the lights sparkling in the fir tree. Not for long, however. George, having chewed his catnip, chose to fly around the room on top of the furniture. After a small figurine on a side table hit the floor when he skidded out of control, I removed the breakables from his path.

"How long do you think it'll take him to sober up?" Ben asked.

I didn't get a chance to answer. George streaked across the couch, knocking the book out of my hands. By the time I bent down to pick it up, he was on his next lap around the room and used my back as a launching pad to the top of the piano.

"Somebody should arrest that cat for reckless driving," I said, removing myself from George's orbit and rubbing the claw indentations in my back.

"Or for contravening the federal laws on low-flying aircraft." Ben tried to catch George on his next fly-by and missed. "Why don't you play hide-and-seek with him? He's in the mood to be silly."

The hide-and-seek game had begun a few weeks earlier. I'd wait until George was asleep, then hide behind the bedroom door and call him. When he walked past the edge of the door, looking for me, I'd pop my head out and say "Boo!" George would start, flatten his ears and stalk away, tail lashing. He never fell for it twice in an evening, but I 'got' him, on average, once a week.

"It won't work unless he's asleep. How about another brandy? I've got time for one more chapter of this murder mystery before supper." Henry cuddled into my lap and purred his approval.

"Good idea. Where's George gone?"

"Probably to sleep it off. He wants to be in good shape for supper since you've made chicken for him."

Half an hour later I was roused from my mystery by George summoning me imperiously from the kitchen. "I wonder what he wants. He knows it isn't time to eat yet."

"My fault," Ben said. "I forgot to give him his treats at noon. He's hungry."

I lifted Henry from my lap, dropped the book and rose. "I'm coming, George. And we'll give the Houseboy ten lashes with a wet noodle."

As I stepped through the doorway into the dark kitchen, George jumped at me and bellowed. I yelped and jerked back in surprise. He smiled with immense satisfaction and strolled into the living room with a triumphant waggle of his behind.

"Serves you right," Ben said, as I settled down with my book again.

I'd read perhaps two words when the sound of a tree ornament hitting the floor made me look up. George was standing on his hind feet and reaching into the branches for another one.

"George! No!"

He ignored me, but Henry jumped off my lap and went over to see what the King was doing. He began pulling coloured balls off the branches, too.

"Listen, you two!"

"Oh, just ignore them," Ben said. "They'll get bored after awhile."

It didn't look as though boredom would set in any time soon. Once they'd taken all the ornaments off the bottom branches they spent the next half hour batting them to the far corners of the house. When I couldn't stand it any longer, I distracted the two deconstruction experts with dishes of chicken and rehung the ornaments.

After supper George and Henry learned how to reach the higher branches. Henry stood on the end of the couch and snagged coloured balls from there; George was balanced precariously on top of the piano, swiping at ornaments with one paw. The tree was half denuded.

I gathered up the ornaments and hid them in a box. "I'll put them back in the morning," I said. "Maybe by that time the cats will have forgotten this game."

At eight, Cal Peterson wandered in to have a pre-Christmas drink with us. "How come you only decorated part of the tree?"

George and Henry, looking as if butter wouldn't melt in their mouths, sat solemn and dignified in front of the tree, pretending they weren't a bit interested in it.

When I explained that the cats had taken down most of the ornaments, Cal shook his head. "They couldn't reach the top of the tree," he said. "If you've run out of things to put on it, I've got some I can loan you."

***

On Boxing Day, Ben came in from feeding the deer, his face white and a sopping wet Nicky in his arms. "That swimming pool has to go. Now."

"What happened?"

"Nicky was trying to herd the deer. A doe escaped him, leapt onto the cover and ripped a hole in it with one of her sharp hooves."

"Is she all right? Did she get out?"

"Nicky went after her and she managed to jump to the apron. We're lucky that pool cover is so strong. We're lucky she didn't rip more holes and fall right in. We're lucky Nicky didn't drown when he fell in."

I found an old bath towel and began rubbing Nicky dry. "He's a good swimmer."

"I know, but that water is really cold," said St. Francis, pacing back and forth. "And what if the cats had been out there? You know how clumsy Henry is; he could fall in the pool without half trying."

"Maybe you could build a fence around it." As much as I wanted to see the pool gone, I hated to see Ben deprived of his fun.

"That thing has already cost too much money; there's no point wasting more on it." Ben shook his head. "I hate to see the pool go, Holly, but having it there is too dangerous for the animals."

I said, "We could go down to the beach on sunny days; it's barely a quarter mile away." Or could if we were still living here come summer, which I doubted.

"Four-tenths of a kilometre. And Nicky likes the sea. Once the pool is filled in, we could put concrete tile over the whole area. Then put a wrought iron table and benches and big pots of flowers on it, like a detached patio. We could still sit out there after I have my swim in the sea."

"Can we put a border of rhododendrons or roses around the perimeter? And build a little fountain?"

"Sure!" Ben began to look enthusiastic. "You know, the sale of all the pool equipment might even pay for filling the hole and building the patio." He went off to play with his budget.

Soon the pool had been drained and several truckloads of rock dumped in the bottom, along with gravel and soil. Ben put an ad in the local paper for motors and pumps and various other equipment we'd inherited with the property. The pool was gone.

"We'll have to put more gravel and soil in when that settles," Ben said. "It'll be a while before we can do the concrete tile, but at least none of the animals will get hurt now." He eyed the beginnings of our new patio. "If we had lots of money, I'd build a Roman bath there, with a caldarium, a tepidarium and a frigidarium."

"What are those for?"

"Can't you guess? The caldarium is the hot tub, the tepidarium is to cool off in, and the frigidarium is the cold plunge before you go to the massage room."

"We'd have to hire a masseuse, too."

"We've already got two of those. The cats walk all over us every chance they get."

***

Three days after Christmas, we left George's empire in Cal's hands and took the ferry to Victoria. Most of our friends were away or playing host to out of town relatives so we booked into a bed and breakfast near the city centre and settled in for a long anticipated mini-holiday.

On New Year's Eve day, I drove to Aunt Peggy's house and told my tenants they'd probably have to move out by March or April. Our two years on the farm were almost up.

The Mitchells looked glum. Bob said, "We were hoping we could stay forever, weren't we, Anne?"

His wife nodded. "We've always loved old houses. Come upstairs and see what Bob's done with the front bedroom."

What Bob had done was wallpaper and furnish it in the style of the 1920's. The room was stunning and I said so. I was just about to say I would reimburse him for his time and materials when I realized I was visualizing the upstairs front bedroom at the farm done the same way. How odd! I went over to the window and stared down at the traffic zooming by while more odd thoughts drifted through my mind.

***

Rusty, Ben's ex-boss, had invited us to his house to celebrate the new year. When his wife, Jean, opened the door, the first thing she said was, "Well, have you sold the farm?"

"No," I said, "not yet. And it's two years since you bet we wouldn't last a year."

"Has it been that long? I was sure you'd be back in civilization long before now."

Rusty poured drinks and Jean dropped a fifty dollar bill in my lap. "What will you buy with your winnings?"

"If we could ever find the right name for the farm, I'd get a sign made for the gate," Ben said.

"What about 'Sutton's Sanctuary'?" Rusty handed Ben a beer.

"Too many esses," Ben said. "Too long. Anyway, we thought we might name it after George or Henry."

"How about George's View?" Jean said.

Ben said, "Sounds too much like Georgia View. With hundreds of miles of coastline bordering the Georgia Strait, can you imagine how many places are called 'Georgia View'?"

"I'd suggest Cat House," Jean said, "But I don't suppose that stands a chance."

When midnight came, we still hadn't thought of a name, but by that time it didn't seem to matter. We toasted the New Year and each other and made resolutions.

Rusty said he would play more golf, Jean that she'd lose fifteen pounds. Ben decided he'd experiment with making dandelion or pear wine.

"I'm not going to make any more bets about you staying on the farm, either," Jean said. "What's your resolution, Holly?"

I couldn't admit that I didn't have one. My sudden lack of direction was inexplicable, even to me. "I'm going to get a Siamese kitten."

"Hey," Ben said, "we don't need any more cats!"

"I'm willing to wait until you've incorporated it in the budget." I knew I'd have to wait longer than that. George and Henry didn't bite or claw each other, but a kitten might, in wild playing, get a taste of Henry's blood or saliva and pick up his HIV infection. But there was no harm in preparing Ben and his budgets for a kitten sometime in the future. I hoped, in one way, that it would be a very long time in the future. As Jerry had said, Henry could live for years yet.

Ben eyed me, the corners of his mouth turning up in spite of his attempt to control them. "My budgets are a little more flexible than they used to be. Maybe it's because my station in life has sunk so low that all I can manage is being a houseboy in a royal household."

"You're a what?" Rusty asked.

XXII - MIDNIGHT RAMBLES

I liked being awake after midnight when everything was quiet and still and the rest of the world slept – provided I could go back to sleep when I felt like it. I loved watching the cats glide through patches of moonlight in the yard and disappear into the shadows, intent on mysterious errands. I fantasized doing the same, but knew my clumsy human feet could never match their silent grace.

Sometimes Nicky joined them, but often he merely blinked from his perch at the foot the bed, yawned and went back to sleep. Like Ben, he thought the dark hours were meant for sleep.

Whether I was in the mood for romantic musing or not, I was awake and out of bed at least once during the small hours because Henry wanted to go outside. He refused to use the cat door as adamantly as he refused the litter box. Perhaps he though both were George's private property.

Henry looked robust but the FIV was lurking, making him susceptible to other infections. We didn't like to leave him outside for long, so one of us always got up to let him out and waited until he came in again. On rainy nights his trips took fifteen minutes or so. This was about the right time for a cigarette, a glass of milk, and quiet contemplation of the movie we'd watched after dinner, the next day's tasks, or why I thought cats were wonderful. On dry nights, he didn't want to come in at all and I trotted around the yard looking for him in the dark, hoping I wouldn't step on a twig, a pebble or a slug.

I didn't mind getting up to let him out; it was the way he announced he was ready that irritated me. He'd get all forty-eight claws on the stereo speaker and rake it. He didn't do any real damage, but the loud ripping sound was guaranteed to wake me instantly and have me racing to find out what part of the house the cats were destroying this time.

Worse, he also did it when he wanted permission to eat his dry food. This was maddening because it seemed so illogical. I'd never known a cat that didn't believe he had the right to eat any food – his or ours – whenever he felt like it. And Henry had no doubts about his rights. But there it was – when he headed for the dry food, I had to pat him on the head and say, "It's okay, Henry, you can eat that," before he'd touch a mouthful.

One warm night during the first week of March, Henry roused me, in his usual fashion, at midnight. By the time I'd reached the back door to let him out, I was awake enough to realise he wasn't following me. He was sitting in front of his dry food dish, looking at me expectantly.

"You're a big nuisance." I patted him and told him he was allowed to eat. He began crunching.

Ben awoke as I got into bed. "What are you doing up?"

"Henry wanted permission to eat his dry food. I'm going to kill that cat one of these days."

"If this was ancient Egypt you'd be put to death for even saying that," Ben said sleepily.

"This is not ancient Egypt."

He continued, with increasing enthusiasm. "They thought cats were gods and worshipped them. If you killed one, even by accident, you were stoned to death."

"Persist in your history lessons at midnight," I replied sweetly, "and you will be, too."

"I'll tell you about it tomorrow," he promised and went back to sleep.

I spread the sleeping bag on the couch. If I went back to bed, Henry would only come and dig me out, because another of his rights was to sit on my chest where he could knead until he was in a trance and stare out the living room window – his idea of heaven. I liked to lie there and look at the stars myself. And it was a bonus to escape Ben's snoring.

I settled on the couch and waited for Henry to join me, hoping I'd be asleep before he and George started arguing over which of them owned my hip.

I was drifting off to dreamland when Henry clawed the stereo speaker again.

"Now what?"

He wanted out.

After letting him out, I got a glass of milk, an ashtray and my cigarettes and prepared to stay awake for fifteen minutes. On cue, he came back in and we repaired to the couch and sleep.

At four a.m. Henry scratched the speaker cover again. I didn't want to get up so I let him scratch. After a minute, the speaker cover fell off with a thud, narrowly missing him. He gazed at it in amazement, decided he didn't want anything after all and curled up on my chest again.

At six a.m. the cat door crashed open, waking me, and George galloped in. I closed my eyes again and was almost asleep when a familiar sound brought me upright on the couch, eyes wide open. George was throwing up – into the speaker cover.

I climbed out of the sleeping bag and cleaned up the mess as well as I could, considering I didn't have my glasses on and it wasn't daylight yet. Back in the bag, I shut my eyes and wondered why I'd ever thought cats were marvellous. At six-thirty, Henry scratched the other speaker cover.

"What do you want?" I moaned.

Both he and George stared at me in hurt astonishment. How could I lie there lazing the day away? Didn't I realize it was time for breakfast?

Next day Ben decided he'd do the graveyard shift. "If I don't hear him, just poke me and I'll get up."

This didn't seem very efficient. After all, if I was awake enough to poke Ben, I was awake enough to look after Henry. Why should both of us be awake? However, I agreed to give it a try.

That night Henry scratched the wallpaper beside the bed and, before I could get out from under the covers, Ben sat up and said firmly, "I'll go."

He stomped into the kitchen and turned all the lights on. I hid my head under the pillow. Light bothers my eyes if I'm just waking up and I've always assumed there must be some cat genes in my make-up. Whether my eyes shine in the dark the way cats' eyes do, no one has ever said.

Henry stayed out for a long time. The Houseboy roamed from back door to deck door to front door, opening them and calling, shutting them, turning inside and outside lights on and off. He opened the dishwasher and clattered a few dishes into the cupboard.

He stomped back into the bedroom.

"Do you know that cat's been outside for twenty-eight minutes?" he demanded.

"Mfff."

"What does he do out there?"

"Mfff."

"This is ridiculous! He's got to learn to come back in when he's supposed to."

I wanted to tell him that looking after Henry was not the same as looking after the son Ben raised so well, but even in my half-asleep state, I knew this was not the time.

Ben went back to the kitchen. I heard the back door open and Henry's cheerful "Prrrt!" as he came in, no doubt with jauntily waving tail.

"Don't 'prrrt!' me," growled Ben. "Where've you been?"

"Prrrt!"

Grumbling, Ben came back to bed. Within five minutes, he was snoring.

I spread the sleeping bag on the couch. Henry leapt onto my chest, purring, and proceeded to knead.

"It's okay, sweetie," I said. "You're a big, grown-up cat, not a little kid. You don't need to tell anybody anything. Next time he asks where you've been, say 'Out.' And if he asks what you were doing, say 'Nothing'." Henry kneaded himself into a trance.

I told Ben I'd rather do night duty than lie awake listening to him do it, but he still didn't think it was fair that I should pull all the graveyard shifts.

The pattern was repeated next night. Every time Ben asked Henry a question, the answer was "Prrrt!"

All this chatter meant I was wide awake. Ben came back to bed and said, "Why does Henry stay out so long?"

"He likes being outside."

"But he's got a nice warm house to live in, and soft places to sleep and all the food he can eat."

"So do you, but you still like to go outside."

"That's different; I have things to do."

"So does Henry. He has to check his territory and explore smells and sounds. Besides, cats are still wild in some ways and he enjoys the freedom of the night." It was hard for me to find the right words when I was half asleep. "I love it, too."

Ben was silent for a moment. "Okay, I guess I have been assuming the cats think the way I do. They're so darn smart it's hard to remember they're not human."

"They're not children, either, even if they do look on us as parents when they're inside. Outside, at night, they're adult cats with their own set of instincts and senses, as independent as their wild ancestors were."

"But the cats do resemble humans in a lot of ways." Ben plumped up his pillow. "You say yourself Henry is a Buddhist."

"That's just shorthand. What I'm really saying is that he is like a Buddhist."

"If you're going to quibble about semantics, I'm going to sleep."

The next night, when Henry returned, he'd had an adventure and told the Houseboy all about it in a series of meows and trills.

Ben came back to bed. "What was he talking about?"

"How would I know?"

"Well, you're a Cat Person. You should know."

I rolled over, faked a snore and promised myself that I really would get up and do door duty for Henry from then on. Those complicated questions that Ben came up with in the middle of the night were too hard on a brain that had been in neutral since dinner time.

***

A week later Ben announced that George had been with us two years and Henry one year. "I think we ought to have a little celebration."

"Celebrate what? Our survival?" I was suffering from sleep deprivation.

"Come on, it's not that bad." He could say so, of course, since I was back on night duty for Henry. "We could celebrate their anniversaries by opening a bottle of wine for ourselves and cans of something extra deluxe for all three of the fur people."

The anniversary boys were curled up beside Nicky on the veranda, basking in the sun. In spite of cat hair in the soup, dog hair on the sofa and interrupted sleep, I couldn't imagine life without these furry creatures who'd brought so much wit and playfulness into our lives. They surprised us almost every day with new pranks or cleverness.

"I have another idea," Ben said. "Instead of wine, let's open that bottle of single malt scotch we've been saving for a special occasion."

"You're talking serious celebration."

"I'm talking serious discussion," Ben said.

I'd been waiting for him to say something. Our two years on the farm was up, give or take a week, and it was time to decide whether to stay or move back to Victoria. I knew what I wanted to do.

Ben poured us each a generous measure of the single malt and we toasted the sleeping animals and each other.

"My decision will be a celebration for you, Holly," Ben said. "This market gardening venture won't succeed unless I build a greenhouse and pipe in a reliable source of water. That will cost a bundle and we don't have it."

"We have enough income to live on."

"But not much more than that. We could borrow against the farm, but if we had a bad year, how would we pay the mortgage?"

"So you're saying you want to move back to Victoria?"

"No," Ben said, "I'm not saying that at all. I'd give my right arm to stay here but we made an agreement. I can't make the garden a success unless I spend a lot of money on it and I know you'd rather be in the city. So the experiment has failed on both counts."

He looked so sad that I wanted to comfort him, but I needed answers to a couple of questions first. "Where would you get enough water to keep the garden going?"

"Ken Dyckman's property goes way back up into the hills and there's a fair-sized lake up there. When he started raising cattle, he built a pipeline down to his yard. He told me I could tap into his supply as long as I paid for ditching and piping and all the rest of it."

"How much would it cost? And how much to build a greenhouse?"

Ben gave me a figure. "Why do you want to know? I can't see any point in even discussing it."

I smiled. "Because half of the experiment succeeded. When I was in Aunt Peggy's house at New Year's, I had a sort of revelation. I realized that I'd come to love life on the farm and the island. That I liked my island friends as much as my city friends. That this is home...."

The rest of my words were buried in Ben's shoulder as he wrapped his arms around me and hugged until I was breathless. I felt a drop of moisture on my scalp and nearly burst into tears myself.

"Why didn't you tell me sooner?" Ben demanded.

"Because I wasn't sure. I fought the idea of living on a farm for so many years that I was afraid my revelation was just a momentary blip. It's taken me most of the last three months to accept that I do love this place."

Ben moved away, scowling, and I knew he was trying to disguise the fact that his eyes were still wet. "Are you willing to risk a mortgage then?"

"We don't have to do that," I said. "Last week I phoned my tenants and they're going to buy Aunt Peggy's house. There'll be more than enough money for a pipeline and a greenhouse."

Ben came back and put his hands on my shoulders. "Are you sure? Are you sure you want to spend your inheritance on the farm?"

"Absolutely. But there's one condition."

"Anything at all," he said, draining his glass.

"I want two Siamese kittens."

"Two!" Ben stared at me. "That's blackmail! You said one at New Year's."

"Two will be twice as much fun."

"Uh huh. And double the vet fees, the annual shots and the flea medicine. And double the food." Ben gave a mock groan. "You know what my other New Year's resolution should have been? To do the budget in pencil!"

"But think what all those pencils would cost."

Ben beamed. "Have as many damn kittens as you like. This really is a celebration! Want another scotch?"

"You bet I do! I have two other reasons for celebrating, you know. One is that my two cat poems were accepted. The letter came this morning." I pulled it out of my pocket where I'd hidden it, waiting for an appropriate moment to brag.

He hugged me again and grinned. "That's fantastic! So, are you going to write some more?"

"I might, but now I've got the chance to do some writing and actually get paid for it."

He looked surprised. "You have? Where?"

"I ran into Scott West, the publisher of the Adriana Advocate, in the grocery store the other day. I told him about getting the poems published and he asked me if I'd write a column."

"Wow! That's terrific. Did you say yes?"

"No, but I will now that we've decided to stay here."

"My wife the newspaper reporter," Ben said. "What are you going to write about, the cats?"

"No. The column will be called Tidelines and be about what's happening on the island."

"Gossip, you mean."

"Well, not about who's dating who. More like business gossip, who's selling, who's buying, who's trying to start something new and why, and what I think about it."

"I'll bet you end up writing about the cats."

"I have no idea what I'm going to write about. Which is why I love the idea of this job. Who knows where it will lead me?"

"Wouldn't suit me," Ben said. "I like to know what I'm doing and where I'm going."

"No kidding!" I curled up in my favourite chair. "Now that the farm is a forever thing, it really is time we named the place."

"You've thought of one, haven't you?" Ben said.

"Yes. How about The Funny Farm?" I had to giggle at the horrified look on his face.

"No way!"

"I was only teasing. What about Holly Haven?"

Ben's eyes misted up again. "Is that actually how you feel about it?"

"Yes."

"Then that's what we'll call it. I wonder if Cal could make a sign for us out of cedar."

"He could certainly weave one out of wool."

"Holly, are you sure you need a second scotch?"

"I'm positive. Only I've decided this one won't be for celebration but for drowning my sorrows."

Ben stared at me. "What sorrows?"

"I've had to give up my dreams of being Head Cat. His Supreme Majesty, Georgius Felinus Rex, refuses to recognize my status. How am I going to survive another ten or fifteen years as a mere head slave?"

Ben looked thoughtfully at our sleeping friends. "And I doubt I'll ever be anything but a lowly houseboy."

"So are you going to pour another scotch?"

"I think we deserve it. But, on second thought, I'm not so sure about giving the royals a deluxe dinner. After all, George still owes us for a set of curtains."